Diplomacy, Trade, and South Korea's Rise to International Influence

LEXINGTON STUDIES ON KOREA'S PLACE IN INTERNATIONAL RELATIONS

Series Editor: Jongwoo Han, Syracuse University

This series publishes trailblazing research by pioneering scholars on contemporary Korean issues. Transformative events in the early twenty-first century have marked a watershed for South and North Korea in many areas, including political economy, democracy, international power politics and security, ongoing disputes over the past with China and Japan, and North Korea's nuclear and missile programs, to name a few. Furthermore, post-modern cultural influences and the global advent of digital technology have led to the diversification of Korea's culture, religion, sports, diasporic community, and inter-Korean linguistic differences, as well as the Korean Wave. This series aims to explore and dissect these issues to further understanding of contemporary Korean life and politics.

Recent Titles in This Series

Korea and the World: New Frontier in Korean Studies
Edited by Gregg Brazinsky
Diplomacy, Trade, and South Korea's Rise to International Influence
by Dennis Patterson and Jangsup Choi

Diplomacy, Trade, and South Korea's Rise to International Influence

Dennis Patterson and Jangsup Choi

LEXINGTON BOOKS
Lanham • Boulder • New York • London

Published by Lexington Books
An imprint of The Rowman & Littlefield Publishing Group, Inc.
4501 Forbes Boulevard, Suite 200, Lanham, Maryland 20706
www.rowman.com

6 Tinworth Street, London SE11 5AL, United Kingdom

British Library Cataloguing in Publication Information Available

Library of Congress Cataloging-in-Publication Data

ISBN 9781498583084 (cloth)
ISBN 9781498583107 (pbk.)
ISBN 9781498583091 (electronic)

Contents

Figures and Tables

FIGURES

TABLES

Acknowledgments

The authors express their sincere thanks to the Academy of Korean Studies for its support of this project. Also, our thanks goes to Professor Uk Heo and his staff at the University of Wisconsin, Milwaukee for hosting the "South Korea's Rise in a Globalized World" conferences at which we received valuable feedback on parts of this book. This research was supported by a grant from the Academy of Korean Studies (KSPS) funded by the Korean Government (MEST) (AKS-2012-AAZ-2101).

Chapter One

South Korea's Post-Armistice Rise to Prosperity and International Influence

South Korea is an advanced democracy that has become increasingly influential in international affairs, and this is true for both economic and political reasons. Economically, South Korea's rapid economic growth in the post-armistice period pulled the country out of abject poverty and near complete dependence and turned it into a member of world's developed nations, exporting well-known, high-quality goods and capital. Moreover, its transformation from one of the world's poorest nations to a country with the world's eleventh largest economy has rendered it a model of economic development to be emulated by the world's less developed economies. In addition to South Korea's remarkable economic achievements, this nation has, at the same time, registered a significant number of international political achievements. These include South Korea successfully transitioning from authoritarianism to democracy as well as becoming an increasingly important diplomatic power, securing memberships in a large number of the world's most important international organizations. These include the prestigious Development Assistance Committee (DAC) of the Organization for Economic Cooperation and Development (OECD), which means that South Korea has become a full partner in the family of "middle power" nations, exerting a growing influence in global affairs.[1]

South Korea's ascendance to its current level of international influence as a relatively new "middle power" is a remarkable story not just because of the sheer magnitude of the transformation it experienced—something that is nearly unmatched by any other nation in history—but also because the initial conditions from which it arose were so inauspicious.[2] When the Korean War ended, South Korea had virtually no industry and whatever industrial capacity and economic infrastructure it did possess was destroyed by the invasion of the North Korean army. As a result, it was completely dependent on largesse from the United States, so much so that the government of its first post-independence president, Rhee Syngman, would have collapsed without the substantial infusions of money it received from the United States. The conditions it faced at this time led *New York Times* reporter A. M. Rosenthal, to conclude that South Korea's future was "dreary" and that it would remain poor and dependent on the United States ". . . for the foreseeable future, perhaps for decades."[3]

We know well that South Korea's inauspicious beginnings in the post-armistice period were overcome by its leaders, whose efforts began producing positive results as early as the middle- to late-1960s, and we also know that they have continued to the present day. As a result, South Korea's dramatic transformation from poverty and dependence to prosperity and international influence has increasingly behooved scholars to examine and explain this country's remarkable transformation. The explanations we currently have for South Korea's rise to its current position of international influence have certainly brought to light many features of its transformation that were inadequately treated in the past. Naturally, different scholarly works have emphasized different aspects of South Korea's international rise, but, in spite of this, all scholarly work on this topic is characterized by a single underlying theme that rests on the role played by South Korea's rapid economic growth later in the post-armistice period.

South Korea's rapid economic growth has indisputably proven to be a worthy topic for scholarly investigation, and we know from existing work that it certainly helped raise South Korea's international status. The problem is that it has been elevated in the scholarly literature to the status of principal explanatory factor for South Korea's becoming the internationally influential "middle power" it is today. What this has done is not simply misconstrue the role that rapid economic growth actually played in South Korea's transformation and international rise,[4] but it has also led scholars to leave out other important factors that are necessary for a complete explanation of this important phenomenon.[5] The result is that there is still something missing in our understanding of how this once poor, isolated, and dependent nation managed to achieve all that it did in such a short period of time.[6]

The problem is that by assuming, either explicitly or implicitly, that it was South Korea's rapid economic growth that drove its rise to international influence, scholars have missed how far along the path to elevating its international status this country was before rapid growth kicked in and accelerated this process. To be sure, we are not saying that rapid economic growth was unimportant because, without rapid economic growth, South Korea would not have become the internationally influential actor it is today, molding the policies of many of the world's most important international organizations.

As stated briefly above, South Korea is a member of the OECD's important Development Assistance Committee (DAC), the policy-making body of the world's leading donor nations, because it has come to possess sufficient wealth to be an important distributor of Official Development Assistance (ODA) itself. Rather, the problem is that this emphasis leads scholars to miss all the important international achievements that South Korea's leaders realized before it became the prosperous nation it is today. As a result, there is so much more to how the Republic of Korea became the influential international actor it is today than is suggested by existing scholarship.[7]

The fact is that South Korea's path to international influence began long before it earned its well-deserved reputation for being a model of economic development for the world's developing nations. One reason for this is that, early in the post-armistice period, South Korea's leaders struggled to end the isolation their nation found itself in at the end of the Korean War and reconnect it to the world. The efforts of South Korea's leaders during the early years of the post-armistice period not only allowed their nation to establish formal diplomatic connections with an increasingly large number of nations, they also set their country on the path to international influence in both direct and indirect ways. They directly elevated South Korea's international status simply by connecting it formally with more and more of the world's countries and international organizations. They indirectly put South Korea on the path to international influence by helping its companies find international trade connections, which in turn led to a significant growth in the country's exports, and ultimately stimulated its rapid economic growth.

Once again, we are not relegating the role played by South Korea's remarkable economic development in its post-armistice rise because its economic transformation helps explain how its growing international influence accelerated, especially in the last two to three decades. Rather, the point is that South Korea's rapid economic development itself cannot account for the international successes it experienced during the years of the Cold War simply because they occurred when South Korea was still a poor country. This means that an essential part of the explanation for South Korea's international rise rests with how its leaders used the tools of diplomacy to remove it from the near complete isolation and utter dependence it found itself in when the armistice ending the Korean War was promulgated in 1953.

This point does not mean that historians and political scientists have completely ignored the diplomatic efforts of South Korea's leaders in the years before rapid economic growth because, as we discuss in more detail below, there are numerous treatments of South Korea's relations with select nations of the world at different times throughout the years of the Cold War. Rather, the issue is that they have not been given these diplomatic efforts the weight they deserve in explaining South Korea's rise to international influence. The diplomatic successes of South Korea's leaders earlier in the post-armistice period, particularly those of President Park Chung-Hee, contributed greatly to this nation's ascendance in international status in more than one way. Successful efforts in the early post-armistice period to establish formal connections to a growing number of nations helped South Korea make gains in its international legitimacy, which was quite challenged by the very rigid alliance structure of the Cold War world.[8] Successful diplomatic efforts also laid the ground work not just for further diplomatic gains and the growing number of formal connections South Korea would establish, they also helped this nation become increasingly involved in a number of international bodies and forums, paving the way for eventual full-fledged membership in many important international organizations.

In these ways, the diplomatic efforts of leaders in early post-armistice South Korea helped directly to elevate its international status, but, as suggested above, they also helped South Korea's leaders put the country on the path to international influence in one other way. South Korea's diplomatic gains in the early post-armistice period formed an essential component of the economic policy that ultimately led to its rapid economic growth. Studies of South Korea's economic development, be they very recent or appearing two or more decades ago,[9] have emphasized how government policies facilitated that country's rapid economic growth by making export-led growth the focus of the policy effort.[10] Studies have noted that it was gains in South Korea's international trade—exports in particular—that helped pull along the remarkable rise in its per capita GDP that occurred in the post-armistice period. The data are very telling here as, at the beginning of the Cold War, South Korea's international trade was negligible but increased to $300 million in 1960. Ten years later, South Korea's international trade had grown over 900 percent to $3 billion. While this is a significant increase, the rate of growth in South Korea's international trade increased by 1000 percent in the next decade, and, while, after this, the rate of increase did decline, the value of South Korea's combined exports and imports continued to climb and stands at a total trade volume of over $1 trillion today (see the data and discussion presented in chapter 5).

What is most important for our purposes here is that the increases in international trade that occurred in the early decades of the post-armistice period are essentially taken for granted in studies of South Korea's economic development. What this means is that explanations of Korea's international trade are merely assumed to be the byproduct of the domestic policies that went into designing and implementing South Korea's export-led economic development strategy.[11] What is missing is the very important point that an export-led growth policy cannot occur when a nation is as internationally isolated and as economically dependent as South Korea was at the end of the Korean War. South Korea's leaders needed to take action that would overcome the international constraints their nation faced and help establish long-term export markets and find dependable suppliers of needed imports. To accomplish these goals, South Korea's leaders needed to establish secure and friendly relations with the governments of those nations that would become trading partners, and this would require strategically targeted diplomatic efforts.[12]

At the beginning of the post-armistice period, Cold War divisions and intense competition from its adversary in the north helped contribute to South Korea's status as an isolated and dependent nation. As a result, it had very few of the stable and friendly diplomatic relations necessary to engage in the level of international trade it needed to effect an export-led economic development strategy. This situation behooved South Korea's leaders to expend much effort on establishing and maintaining diplomatic relations in the Cold War years, not just to increase its own international legitimacy but also to allow its companies to work with counterparts in friendly nations, that is, nations with which South Korea's leaders were able to establish and maintain long-term diplomatic relations. In this way, diplomacy was a necessary tool of the Republic of Korea's development strategy because it encouraged the expansion of its international trade, helping to ensure the success of its export-led development strategy, and reducing risks of disruption once these connections were made.

By not giving sufficient weight to the efforts that South Korea's leaders made to establish and maintain relations with nations around the world, scholars have essentially produced explanations for South Korea's international rise that are incomplete. Our purpose in this volume is to fill this scholarly gap by developing and testing a theoretically informed explanation of how South Korea pulled itself out of the isolation and poverty it experienced after the Korean War and put itself on the path to the prosperity and international influence it currently enjoys. To accomplish this, we will need to focus on the diplomatic efforts of South Korea's leaders in the post-armistice period, noting how diplomatic efforts in the Cold War and post-Cold War periods were designed to address different international imperatives and that, in the periods following the collapse of the Berlin Wall, its leaders had many more financial resources at their disposal, which helped to accelerate the country's process of elevating itself internationally.

What this means is that we essentially turn the argument that economic growth drove South Korea's rise to international influence on its head. Specifically, we proceed from the notion that it was, first, South Korea's diplomatic successes in the Cold War years, successes that occurred without the country being able to buy embassies, as some scholarly works have either implicitly assumed or explicitly asserted,[13] that set the country on the path to greater trade and wealth and, thus, actually led it to ultimately become the important international actor that it currently is. To be clear about how we will proceed, we devote the remainder of this chapter to the content of this volume's remaining chapters.

This effort will begin with a discussion of how South Korea's transformation and rise to international influence has been explained by scholars. In chapter 2, we will summarize this scholarly literature, focusing on how existing treatments, while insightful, are limited in one of two ways. First, they have either taken South Korea's rapid economic growth for granted rather than treated it as an intellectual problem that needs to be unambiguously connected to the country's overall international status or they have offered explanations that simply assume that discussing domestic export promotion policies is sufficient to account for how South Korea actually increased its international connections and, thus, exported volumes. Once we bridge this gap in the scholarship, we will then offer a theoretical perspective that we employ to help develop and test a more complete explanation of how South Korea's leaders put the country on the path to the international influence it enjoys today before rapid economic growth accelerated this process. The theoretical perspective that will inform our explanation for South Korea's international rise is known in international political economy literature as "trade follows the flag," and we employ it in our analysis because of its relevance for understanding how South Korea's leaders built diplomatic relations not only to remove their nation from international isolation but also to help Korean companies build reliable trading connections.

Our discussion of how this theoretical perspective helps us provide a complete explanation for the post-armistice rise of South Korea will take place in two parts. Since our overall argument is that it was the diplomatic efforts of South Korea's leaders that not simply helped reconnect the country to the nations of the world, it was this growing number of diplomatic connections that helped trade expand, allowing the implementation of the country's export-led economic–development strategy. It was in this way that South Korea's leaders put the country on the path to international influence early in the post-armistice period, long before it became the prosperous exporter of capital and high quality goods that it is today. The diplomatic efforts of South Korea's leaders did not cease when the Berlin Wall came down but continued throughout the post-Cold War years, which is the period of time when South Korea's economic growth accelerated, which allowed its leaders to employ more economic resources in their diplomatic activities in a world that was defined by fewer international constraints and, thus, allowed more flexibility in their foreign policy efforts. This discussion of South Korean diplomacy and its economic impacts will take place over two chapters.

In chapter 3, we focus on South Korea's diplomatic efforts during the years of the Cold War and analyze how these efforts led to an expansion of its international trade, which was the foundation of its domestic economic development strategy. South Korea's leaders faced a unique set of international conditions during the Cold War because the international system involved more than just a divided world: it was defined by interstate relations that were hierarchical, placing more constraints on how the world's less powerful nations could build and maintain formal connections with other countries. Despite such constraints, succeeding leaders in South Korea set goals that involved expanding their diplomatic connections, which helped pave the way for the increased international trade South Korea came to enjoy as the post-armistice period progressed.

Despite the international constraints of the Cold War years, South Korea's diplomatic gains helped directly pave the way for the expansion of the country's exports. The post-Cold War years, on the other hand, represent a period where South Korean diplomacy was much less constrained because of changing international conditions and was supported by South Korea's expanding economic wherewithal, which allowed its leaders increasingly to employ the tools of economic statecraft to support its foreign policy efforts. These are the topics we discuss in chapter 4, where we provide several illustrations of South Korea's successful use of its growing economic wherewithal, including how the country increasingly participated in and influenced the operation of important international organizations. Perhaps most important of these is South Korea becoming a member of the Development Assistance Committee (DAC) of the Organization for Economic Cooperation and Development (OECD), which allowed its leaders to use their country's experience as a long-time recipient of economic aid to mold donor policies for the distribution of Official Development Assistance (ODA) so that recipient nations could experience the maximum amount of benefit.

In chapter 5, we conduct a statistical analysis in which we calibrate the importance of South Korea's diplomatic activities on the expansion of its international trade. Specifically, we weigh the influence that South Korean diplomacy had on trade expansion in both the Cold War years and the post-Cold War period. In this analysis, we control for those factors that go into decisions involving whether or not to engage in trading relations with a nation, and these include economic, political, and geostrategic factors that influence these decisions. This analysis will reveal that, while diplomacy remains an important explanatory factor in South Korea's trade expansion, the role played by its economic growth greatly increased in importance. In this chapter we also show how it was the diplomatic successes combined with the expansion of international trade that occurred in both the Cold War and post-Cold War periods that led to South Korea's rapid economic growth and ultimate rise in prosperity.

With South Korea having achieved expanded trade and rapid economic growth, it also witnessed gains in its international status. These began early on in the Cold War years, but they accelerated during the years following the collapse of the Berlin Wall. This is because, from the end of the Cold War to the present, South Korea's leaders have been able to employ their nation's expanding economic resources to support their foreign policy goals. As a result, it is in the post-Cold War period that South Korea became the influential international actor it is today, holding important memberships in a number of international organizations. As a result, we turn to exactly to what extent the diplomatic and economic factors we discussed in the preceding chapters help explain the elevation South Korea experienced in its international status.

This is the task of chapter 6, and our efforts begin with how we calibrate South Korea's international status. The measure we employ is taken from the Correlates of War Diplomatic Exchange Data project because it captures South Korea's actual international achievements as well as how its international achievements can be compared to those of other nations. We use this measure to perform a statistical analysis to show how it was a combination of diplomatic success and the country's increasing economic wherewithal that led to South Korea's rise in international influence. The statistical analysis we perform will include measures of diplomatic success and South Korea's expanding economic resources, and it will also include a number of other factors we include as control variables to be certain that our analysis is not characterized by omitted variable bias and reliably weighs the impacts that economic and diplomatic factors had on South Korea's rise in international status.

Overall, the discussions and analyses we provide in the preceding chapters result in a more complete explanation for South Korea's rise to international influence. With this task completed, we turn next to the future of South Korea's international influence. This is the topic of chapter 7, the volume's concluding chapter, and its purpose will be to show how the diplomatic and economic tools that South Korean leaders employed to make it the influential middle power it is today will be the same tools it employs to maintain its current international influence and meet the regional and global challenges it must address to accomplish this goal. This discussion will include a special emphasis on South Korea's role in East Asian international relations, particularly in the context of the rise of China and an increasingly provocative

Pyongyang, but it will also include South Korea's growing influence on the developing and developed worlds outside of this region.

NOTES

1. For a discussion of the distinguishing features of middle powers, see e.g., Cooper et. al. (1993) and Cooper (1997). The traditional middle powers include Canada, Australia, and the Nordic countries. New middle powers include not only South Korea but also Turkey and Mexico. See e.g., Ikenberry and Mo (2013).

2. Perhaps the only other nation whose development rivals that of South Korea's is that of Japan, which transformed itself from a backward and isolated medieval country in the late Tokugawa period of the mid- to late-nineteenth century, into a powerful, modern nation state by the beginning of the twentieth century.

3. Quoted in Seth (2011), p. 373.

4. By misconstrue, we mean that rapid economic development was assumed to have exerted a positive relationship on South Korea's rise to international influence at a time when such an impact was not possible because rapid economic development had yet to commence.

5. All works that are part of this relevant scholarly literature will be discussed in more detail in the following chapter.

6. The reference here is the period after the Armistice of 1953 was promulgated.

7. We use South Korea and the Republic of Korea interchangeably throughout this book.

8. On legitimacy in international politics, see e.g., Hurd (1999).

9. For a more receipt study, see e.g., Kim and Jaffe (2010) and for studies that appeared earlier, see e.g., Kuznets (1977) and Amsden (1989).

10. This is a particularly important theme in Haggard et. al. (1994).

11. In other words, studies of South Korea's post-armistice economic development do not show how that nation's international trade would not have expanded to the extent it did without the implementation of the domestic policies they all discuss.

12. This is the well-known "trade follows the flag" idea in international political economy. See especially Pollins (1989a and 1989b).

13. As we discuss in more detail in the next chapter, the former is characteristic of Heo and Roehrig (2014) while the latter is characteristic of Newnham (2003) who even uses the phrase "buying embassies" in the title of his article.

Chapter Two

Diplomacy and International Trade in South Korea's Transformation

When hostilities on the Korean Peninsula formally ended in 1953, conditions south of the 38th parallel were miserable to say the least, and observers who witnessed these conditions did not foresee a bright future for South Korea. Indeed, South Korea's early post-armistice leaders faced not only a divided and hostile Cold War world, they also had to confront their own nation's extreme poverty, diplomatic isolation, and almost complete dependence on the United States for security and economic assistance. To be sure, these were very inauspicious beginnings for South Korea, but as is well known, its leaders did overcome these challenges, and the result is South Korea becoming a prosperous, democratic nation that stands shoulder to shoulder with the world's most influential and prosperous middle powers today.[1]

South Korea's dramatic economic and political transformations, and ultimate rise to a position of international influence, have become increasingly attractive topics for scholarly investigation. Most scholarly works thus far have been devoted to examining South Korea's economic transformation from a poor and dependent nation to a prosperous manufacturing powerhouse that exports high-quality products and capital. Indeed, how South Korea's economic transformation occurred is a question that has led many scholars to conclude that it is perhaps the most successful model of development that can be emulated by the world's developing economies.

While no less important, a smaller number of scholarly works has focused on the international aspects of South Korea's dramatic transformation. Many of these works have focused on inter-Korean relations, but they also include focused studies of South Korea's relations with the United States, Japan, China, and the Soviet Union. This literature has also dealt with South Korea's participation in various international organizations and forums such as the G20, APEC, and the Development Assistance Committee (DAC) of the

OECD with a focus not just on how South Korea achieved memberships in such prestigious international organizations but also on how it came to be influential in these organizations, molding their policies and influencing their future trajectories.

While certainly focused on different aspects of South Korea's economic transformation and international rise, taken together, the existing scholarly literature has provided us with a clearer picture of how South Korea pulled itself out of poverty, isolation, and dependence and elevated itself into the prosperous and internationally influential nation it is today. In spite of this, as noted above in chapter 1, we are still without a complete explanation for this country's post-armistice transformation. By incomplete, we mean an explanation that includes all factors that were important in South Korea's rise to international influence and that recognizes the timing of its international achievements when they actually occurred.

This is because treatments of South Korea's international rise tend to focus on the post-Cold War era, a time when South Korea was already a prosperous and industrially advanced nation. As a result, existing literature emphasizes South Korea's expanding economic wherewithal as almost a singular cause of this nation's rise to international influence. What this explanation misses is the numerous and profoundly important achievements South Korea's leaders realized throughout the Cold War years, a time before the nation became the developed and prosperous nation it is today. Thus, only when an explanation includes the essential connection that exists between the diplomatic efforts of South Korean leaders in the early post-armistice period and its rapid economic growth, and how this combination of factors contributed to its international rise to the level of "middle power" influence it enjoys today, will we have a complete explanation of South Korea's international rise.

We realize that criticisms of scholarly works that focused on either the political or international aspects of South Korea's post-armistice transformation are not really justified because authors' intentions were to produce works of limited scope,[2] and not necessarily a scholarly investigation of how South Korea achieved the level of international influence it enjoys today. The same can also be said for the scholarship that exists on South Korea's economic transformation, which has been focused specifically on the domestic economy and policies that were designed and implemented to induce export expansion and encourage economic growth. In spite of this, aspects of both of these separate literatures help inform our efforts to produce a more comprehensive explanation of how South Korea overcame extreme poverty and international isolation to become the prosperous and influential actor it is today. We will make clear below how we will take this scholarly literature and integrate it into a theoretically unified explanation for South Korea's international rise, particularly with respect to the smaller number of scholarly works that attempt to account directly for South Korea's international ascendance.

THE INTERNATIONAL RELATIONS OF SOUTH KOREA

We begin this discussion with a critical review of the scholarly literature on South Korea's international relations and how analyses of its relations with specific nations and regions of the world inform our efforts to develop and test the explanation of South Korea's international rise we present in this volume. This body of scholarly work contains a diverse array of studies on South Korea's relations with North Korea, the United States, the Soviet Union, China, and other nations in the East Asian region. To a lesser extent, it also covers the diplomatic efforts of leaders in Seoul toward other parts of the world like Latin America, Africa, and the Middle East, and it covers the international efforts at different times throughout the post-Armistice period. In spite of this broad range of coverage, two sets of bilateral relations have been most important for South Korea, and the first of these focuses on inter-Korean relations or interactions between Seoul and Pyongyang.

One notable group of scholarly works on inter-Korean relations involves historic treatments that address the division of the Korean Peninsula, or, more accurately, the failure of the great powers at the end of the Pacific War to reunify Korea.[3] Among the topics covered by these historically focused works are how these two states are different politically and economically and how the dynamics of their relations have evolved since the division of the Peninsula.[4] Another group of scholarly works on inter-Korean relations is thematic, which means that representative treatments are focused on specific aspects of inter-Korean relations that scholars have selected for more in-depth investigation. The specific topics that have been addressed are numerous, but most notable are those that focused on such problems as economic cooperation, divided families and visitations, nuclear weapons, and prospects for the country's reunification.[5] Finally, there is a scholarly literature that has focused on North Korea itself, that is, its development as a state, its economy, politics, leadership, and the different political and economic challenges its leadership has faced.[6] Most relevant among these works are those that focus on the international behavior of North Korea, not only with an eye toward explaining its patterns in an attempt to render them more understandable if not predictable, but also with a focus on what its future behavior will be like.[7]

This literature on North Korea is important for our purposes because it highlights the diplomatic constraints that South Korea faced throughout most of the Cold War period. We know well that Korea was divided at the 38th parallel when Japan surrendered and that efforts by the United Nations and the major powers failed to provide a path that could lead to a reunification of the Peninsula. What is much less appreciated is that, in the aftermath of the Armistice of 1953, South Korean leaders faced an increasingly divided Cold War world, which placed significant constraints on their diplomatic efforts to reconnect their nation with the rest of the world. Naturally, these constraints related to the structure of the Cold War world and South Korea's lack of economic wherewithal and consequent dependence on the United States for aid and security. Nonetheless, South Korea's leaders early in the aftermath of the Korean War worked to establish diplomatic relations with as many nations as they could and end their nation's international isolation.

While South Korea's diplomatic efforts were increasingly motivated by the desire to connect economically with nations so as to expand its trading relations, it was initially driven by the fact that South Korea's early post-armistice diplomacy had to be conducted in competition with a hostile state in the north. This is important because both North and South Korea competed for international legitimacy, which meant that South Korea's leaders had to establish diplomatic relations with the nations it chose to associate, knowing that North Korea was doing the same. North and South Korea then were in diplomatic competition over which nation would possess the most international legitimacy but more importantly because of the essential role assigned to the United Nations early on in adjudicating the reunification of the Korean Peninsula.

After hostilities ended in the Korean War, both Pyongyang and Seoul were forced to pursue their diplomatic goals while adhering to the Peninsula's version of the Hallstein Doctrine.[8] This meant that both North and South Korea claimed to be the only legitimate government on the Korean Peninsula, and, thus, any country establishing diplomatic relations with one could not then establish diplomatic relations with the other. Consequently, achieving diplomatic contacts outside their larger NATO and Communist blocs took on a zero-sum quality for these nations. As the post-armistice period progressed, however, more countries freed themselves from their colonial status and became independent nations, making themselves available for formal diplomatic relations. This increased the diplomatic competition that existed in inter-Korean relations, leading ultimately to leaders of both countries courting the diplomatic favor of nations that were not formally part of their respective Cold War camps, including a number of countries that joined the increasingly important movement of nonaligned nations.[9] As the Cold War came to a close, however, Seoul's economic progress became a symbol of the South Korean state's success while the repression and economic trouble faced by the North became a symbol of Pyongyang's bankrupt regime.

The other primary diplomatic relationship for South Korea was that with the United States, which has functioned as a provider of aid and security to South Korea, especially earlier in the post-armistice period. Scholars have addressed this essential bilateral relationship on its own, and they have also examined it in the context of United States' relations with Japan and, closer to the end of the Cold War, China and the Soviet Union and those nations that succeeded its collapse.[10] South Korea's bilateral—and multilateral—relations with the United States and the other nations of Northeast Asia have not remained static throughout the post-armistice period, and their dynamics have been very important for the state of and stability in the international relations of Northeast Asia.

They are important for our purposes because the United States' relationship with South Korea has been so influential in the diplomatic affairs of Seoul. One notable illustration of this would be U.S. efforts to encourage a rapprochement between South Korea and Japan and how these efforts led to Japan eventually replacing the United States at the primary provider of Official Development Assistance to South Korea.[11] The relationship between the United States and South Korea has evolved to be sure. Indeed, as the post-Armistice period progressed, South Korea contributed more and more to its own security, while at the same time, pursuing a more independent diplomacy consistent with South Korea evolving into an increasingly important and influential "middle power."[12] Part of this increasingly independent diplomacy involved South Korea pursuing relationships with nations that were formerly communist as well as with those that remained committed to their communist political and economic systems.

South Korea's attempts to establish relations with current and former communist nations is an important part of the story of its rise to international influence, and, as scholars have noted, such efforts began during the later years of the Cold War. Ahn (1980) offered a brief history of South Korea's approach to the communist world and how its approach evolved throughout the years of the Cold War. He notes that South Korea's Cold War diplomatic policy began with its leaders pursuing a strict non-interaction course with any country governed by a communist political system. As the Cold War progressed, however, Ahn (1980) highlights how this strict non-interaction policy was relaxed and the government in Seoul allowed scholarly and cultural contacts with such communist nations as China and the Soviet Union.[13]

This discussion of Seoul's relations with the communist world was extended in Kihl (1991), who noted that the end of the Cold War offered new opportunities for South Korea to establish diplomatic relations with nations with which it remained unconnected. These countries included erstwhile communist nations that made the transition to democratic politics and market economics, such as former Soviet Bloc nations in Eastern Europe as well as those countries that continued to be communist, like Vietnam. The most important diplomatic relationship South Korea's leaders pursued with a communist country is that of China, which has become an increasingly powerful nation in the region. Ye (2017) has noted that Sino-South Korean relations have clearly become closer, especially with respect to trade relations as well as educational and cultural exchanges. Nonetheless, South Korea's bilateral relations with China remain complicated, especially in light of China remaining North Korea's most important ally and South Korea's continuing diplomatic and security relationship with the United States, China's principal adversary.

A related focus in the scholarly literature involves South Korea's leaders pursuing diplomatic relations with nations in the non-communist world. Early in the post-armistice period, establishing formal diplomatic relations with non-communist nations was essential not just because it helped South Korea's leaders continue to remove their nation from international isolation and reconnect with the rest of the world but also because establishing political and economic relations with these countries would help increase the support that South Korea had among voting members of the United Nations.[14] This was particularly true early in the Cold War years because support for the North Korean position increased in the 1960s and early in the 1970s. This development prompted South Korea's leaders to do what they could to establish diplomatic relations with nations that would be sympathetic with Seoul's international position vis-à-vis the North, and, as a result, its leaders sought formal diplomatic relations with such nations as those in Latin America that were supported by the United States. The international imperatives it faced also encouraged South Korea's leaders to investigate establishing relations even with nations that might be inclined to gravitate toward Pyongyang, such as those countries that were affiliated with the Non-Aligned Group of Nations. Naturally, such efforts did help South Korea in its competition with the North, but, as we explain in more detail below, it also helped to lay the groundwork for the rapid growth in international trade South Korea would experience from the late 1970s to the present.

Another focus in the scholarly literature refers to leaders in Seoul participating in select international forums and seeking memberships in the world's most important international organizations. We know that building diplomatic relations with as many nations around the globe as possible was important both to help South Korea's leaders build their nation's international legitimacy and to establish connections with nations that would become part of South Korea's expanding export and import markets. We also know that diplomatic connections and economic development alone do not translate directly into international influence as an emerging "middle power," and, thus, for South Korea to elevate itself to a higher level of international influence, its leaders would have to add international organizations and forums to their diplomatic goals. Specifically, in the late-Cold War and post-Cold War periods, South Korea's leaders began using the country's diplomatic connections and increasing economic wherewithal not only to seek and obtain memberships in the world's most important international organizations and forums but also to influence the policies and actual practices of those international organizations and forums.

While it was after the Berlin Wall came down that South Korea made its greatest strides to becoming an influential member of the world's most important international organizations, the ability of South Korea's leaders to realize such notable achievements as joining the OECD's Development Assistance Committee (DAC), traces its roots to the Cold War years. This is important because, while the scholarly literature does deal with South Korea's rise to international influence, including its memberships in and influence on the international organizations it joined, its focus has been the post-Cold War period and not the international achievements its leaders realized earlier in the post-Armistice period.

Perhaps the best illustration of this is found in Ikenberry and Mo (2013), who provide excellent discussions of South Korea's achievements with respect to gaining memberships in and having influence on the practices of a number of international organizations. Indeed, they focus on such developments as South Korea's role in the development of the G20, its contributions to international finance and economic development policies so that it is balanced and sustainable, and its efforts in the area of international peace and security. These are very important accomplishments for South Korea, which Ikenberry and Mo (2013) make clear in their essays, but because they focus on post-Cold War period in general and the presidency of Lee Myung-Bak in particular, they have selected out a period of time when the strength of South Korea's international influence became undeniable. As a result, they do not trace those underlying factors that allowed the achievements they investigated to occur to their actual origins.

Our purpose is not to criticize the work of Ikenberry and Mo (2013) because it was not intended to address the international efforts of South Korea's efforts prior to the Lee Myung-Bak Presidency. Moreover, the cases they selected to illustrate South Korea's rise to international influence are discussed in a thorough and insightful manner, which again makes it an important contribution to the literature on South Korea's rise to a position of international influence. Nonetheless, it does provide a context for us not only to confirm how South Korea's rapid economic growth undoubtedly helped accelerate its rise to international influence but also to demonstrate that its leaders put it on this path long before it became the prosperous "middle power" it is today. The same context is witnessed in the book by Heo and Roehrig (2014), albeit for somewhat different reasons.

Heo and Roehrig's (2014) book on South Korea's rise is comprehensive in its coverage and, thus, intended to provide a complete explanation for South Korea's rise to international influence. These authors do provide brief but thorough histories of South Korea's diplomatic connections with the nations of the world's principal regions as well as more focused discussions of this country's relations with the world's major powers. These chapter-based discussions of South Korea's growing number of diplomatic connections in both the Cold War and post-Cold War periods, and its consequent growing international influence, are insightful and full of information. The same must also be said for their discussion of South Korea's growing influence in the world's international organizations, which covers the entire post-armistice period but concentrates on developments from the 1990s to the present.

Despite these distinctions, the more focused work of Ikenberry and Mo (2013) is similar to the broadly gauged discussion in Heo and Roehrig (2014) in terms of the underlying assumption that had guided their respective discussions. While more implied in Ikenberry and Mo (2013) but stated explicitly in Heo and Roehrig (2014), the guiding maxim of these scholarly works is that it was South Korea's rapid economic development that was the principal cause of its diplomatic accomplishments and, thus, rise to international influence. Clearly, economic development affects a nation's foreign policy for a number of reasons as Heo and Roehrig (2014) have noted.[15] Moreover, South Korea would not have been able to achieve the level of influence it has in such international organizations as the G20 or the Development Assistance Committee (DAC) of the OECD without it having elevated its economy to the high level of economic development it has achieved. Nonetheless, there is still something missing in these and other scholarly efforts to explain the rise of South Korea to its current position of international influence.

The assumption that, without having achieved the level of economic development it ultimately achieved, South Korea would not have risen to the level of international influence it currently possesses is only partially true. This is because an explanation based on this assumption cannot subsume developments that occurred earlier in the post-armistice period. In other words, this argument is temporally limited in that most of South Korea's diplomatic relations, connections that are thoroughly discussed in Heo and Roehrig (2014), were achieved before it came to enjoy anything near the economic prosperity it currently enjoys. Indeed, its current level of economic wherewithal has certainly assisted its leaders in gaining memberships in and influencing the practices of the G20 and the DAC of the OECD, but it cannot account for the country's diplomatic successes in the Cold War period, especially the early years of that period. This problem of temporal limits is perhaps most aptly illustrated in the argument made by Newnham (2002), whose principal assertion is that South Korea simply purchased embassies in establishing its diplomatic connections. Again, the problem with this assertion is that South Korea had about two-thirds of its post-armistice diplomatic connections long before it was prosperous enough to "buy" embassies.

This problem also applies to the more broadly focused treatment of South Korea's rise in Heo and Roehrig (2014). The issue is not that they have mistakenly asserted that a nation's foreign policy is affected by its level of economic development and overall prosperity because this is true and for the exact reasons that Heo and Roehrig (2014) stipulate. Nonetheless, Heo and Roehrig (2014) treat this relationship very generally and never concretely tie the diplomatic achievements of South Korea's leaders to any of these ways that they argue economic development influences a nation's foreign policy.[16] This is a weakness of this important scholarly effort, but it is not the principal weakness of their explanation. Rather, that rests with the fact that so many of the diplomatic developments achieved by South Korea's leaders that Heo and Roehrig (2014) discuss in detail in their book were accomplished before the country became the economically prosperous nation it is today. What this means is that about two-thirds of South Korea's diplomatic connections cannot be explained by the specific ways that economic development can affect a nation's foreign policy. Consequently, most of South Korea's international political achievements are in a sense taken for granted by Heo and Roehrig (2014).

SOUTH KOREA'S ECONOMIC TRANSFORMATION

While the history and status of South Korea's relations with the nations of the world has received attention from historians and political scientists, it is this nation's economic transformation from poverty to prosperity that has been the primary topic of scholars' attention. This is understandable because South Korea's rapid economic development is an incredibly important problem to be addressed, and it played a very important role in the country's becoming an internationally influential middle power. Scholarly treatments of South Korea's rapid economic development are characterized by certain themes that naturally help account for its dramatic economic transformation, and the themes that define this scholarly literature also help reveal some of the elements that are missing in explanations for how its high levels of economic growth and increasing prosperity are connected to its rise to international influence. This is true for both older works in the literature as well as more recent scholarly treatments of the South Korean economy in the post-armistice period.

Earlier scholarly works on the economic development of South Korea were completed when the country's dynamic economy was just entering the period of high growth and, thus, were published before it became the prosperous and internationally influential middle power it is today. While there are many treatments of South Korea's economic rise, among the two most notable of the early assessments are Kuznets (1977) and Amsden (1989). The former is a more traditional economic analysis of South Korea's economic development, which was completed well before rates of economic growth reached the truly rapid levels we witnessed in the 1980s and 1990s. Amsden (1989), on the other hand, appeared a dozen years later when the country had begun to experience rapid economic growth and was solidly on the path to prosperity. Because they were completed when South Korea's economy was in two different stages of development, they are naturally distinct in tone and emphasis, and perhaps the best way to capture their distinctions is to note that Kuznets (1977) emphasized what South Korean leaders needed to do while Amsden (1989) emphasized what they had done.

In spite of this, these works are similar in that they—like scholarly works on South Korea's economic transformation that were to follow—generally agree that South Korea's growth was export led and that this was possible because of the growth policies designed and implemented by such governments as that led by President Park Chung-Hee. Consequently, they emphasize domestic economic policies and certain socioeconomic and political factors in their discussions of South Korea's export-led growth. This was very true of Amsden (1989), albeit less so for Kuznets (1977), but it very aptly characterizes newer work, despite the fact that recent scholarly works are also distinct from one another.

For example, Myung Oak Kim and Sam Jaffe's (2010) recent volume is focused on what has become known as the "miracle on the Han,"[17] and it is a descriptive work that contains case studies of illustrative industries, like Samsung and LG, which stand out as symbols of South Korea's international economic status and power. This is somewhat different from the work of Chung (2007), which is almost entirely focused on the domestic aspects of this country's economic development and covers topics like investment, domestic savings, and finance, focusing less on government policies. Moreover, Eichengreen et. al., (2012) looked at the structural changes that occurred with South Korea's economic development. It covers some topics that the other volumes cover, and it also has a chapter on economic growth. Finally, there is the work by Mo and Weingast (2013), which uses the concepts of how South Korea evolved an "open access" status in its economy and, ultimately, in its politics to explain the rapid economic development that occurred in the post-armistice period.[18]

While not a comprehensive listing of past and recent scholarship on South Korea's economic transformation,[19] these scholarly investigations are directly important for our purposes here because of how they reveal what is missing in current treatments of how South Korea's diplomatic successes connected to its rapid economic growth. Even though these scholarly works are guided by different theoretical frameworks and focus on different aspects of South Korea's economic transformation, they are similar in their agreement that the expansion of exports was an essential factor in South Korea's becoming a prosperous nation. Moreover, while there are variations in the discussions of how the state helped promote South Korea's exports and, as a result, economic development and increasing prosperity, no one would disagree that it was the policies of the government of President Park Chung-Hee that set in motion the processes that helped South Korea's international trade take off. As a result, all of these works focus on domestic policies, which means that what is missing might be called the international political economy aspect of South Korea's trade take off.

In contrast to this, the argument we make here is that it was the efforts of President Park and his successors to build South Korea's diplomatic relations that facilitated the rapid growth that occurred in its international trade. As stated briefly above, when the armistice that ended the Korean War was first promulgated, South Korea was an internationally isolated nation. It was utterly reliant on the United States, and it had virtually no formal relations with nations other than the United States. Consequently, to implement an export-led economic development strategy, its leaders would need to expand its trading relations, and its leaders used the tools of diplomacy to connect with those countries with which it would eventually establish trading relations. In other words, what scholarship on South Korea's economic transformation has not sufficiently explicated is how it was the diplomatic success of South Korea's leaders that paved the way for its expanding trading relations, thereby making the export-led part of its domestic economic development strategy possible.

Establishing and maintaining formal diplomatic connections is a process that involves significant costs to the nation that seeks to initiate and continue such relations. Rose (2007) has noted that the United States spent $42 billion in 2004 for its diplomatic and consular missions, and, in addition to this, the maintenance of foreign offices requires other expenses such as providing security to all a nation's diplomatic and consular officials. Clearly, nations are willing to absorb these costs because establishing and maintaining diplomatic relations returns benefits to the sending nation, and they also allow sending nations to become connected to global affairs, elevating their respective standing among the nations of the world. These are important benefits to be sure, but establishing and maintaining diplomatic formal relations is partner to another set of payoffs.

The extensive network of today's diplomatic relations, composed of many different nations, suggests that the benefits of formal diplomatic relationships go beyond the reputational payoffs and communication and information advantages naturally associated with nations' diplomatic efforts. Existing research has shown that the diplomatic activities of nations also come with economic benefits, and this is why nations like the United States also include economic motivations in their statements about why they expend the significant sums they do to establish and maintain diplomatic and consular missions throughout the world. Rose (2007) noted that the U.S. Department of State includes such activities as "opening markets" and assisting U.S. businesses as being among the activities in which embassy officials will engage. This should not be surprising as U.S. Department of Commerce officials, whose mission is, inter alia, to promote U.S. business interests, work out of embassy and consular offices abroad. Rose (2007) also provides quotes from several other foreign ministries which assert that promoting their respective countries' business interests was among the missions of their respective diplomatic and consular offices.[20]

The idea that nations' use of the tools of diplomacy are an effective way to establish and expand trading relations is well known in the international political economy literature. Pollins (1989a and 1989b) identified and measured how changes in "state-to-state diplomatic relations" affected trade flows between those nations. The empirical connections that he identified were very strong, allowing him to conclude that diplomacy significantly boosted trade between nations with formally established diplomatic relations and that this was true even when controlling for all the standard economic factors that traditionally go into explaining levels of international trade. Pollins (1989a) referred to this as the "trade follows the flag" idea, and he also noted that there are a number of reasons that diplomacy is such an important factor in determining the flow of goods between nations. In addition to Pollins, the work of Ferguson and Forslid (2014) noted that by helping to reduce the "fixed entry costs" to exporters when entering a new nation, the very establishment of embassies leads to expanded trade between pairs of nations with formal diplomatic connections.[21]

When considering the establishment of trading relations, there is no doubt that the nature of the goods to be exported or imported as well as their quality and price are all important factors that help determine in what goods and services and at what levels nations will trade. However, such economic and product-specific factors are not the only ones that nations take into consideration. Nations entering into a trading relationship will want some assurance that they are establishing a connection with a country that will be economically reliable and politically stable in the long term. Having such assurances will minimize risk and help guarantee that business interests are protected. The best method to provide assurances is to keep lines of communication open, and there is no better way for this to occur than to establish and maintain formal diplomatic relations.

While our principal focus is to explore the impact that formal diplomatic relations has had on the level of trade that South Korea conducts with other nations, we will also examine the impact of other factors that help determine the direction and level of trade that occurs between pairs of nations. To be sure, we know that the direction and level of trade between nations will also depend on certain geopolitical factors, whether or not a nation is a member of a free trade area or whether there is a common language between the traders such as the role played by English in the economic relations of the Commonwealth nations or other languages shared by nations with a similar colonial past.[22] There is also the impact of a nation belonging to a currency union, and perhaps the most important example would be that of Europe where transactions take place in Euros.[23] Finally, there is distance, which affects the costs associated with moving goods and services across borders.

By examining the impact of our main variable of interest, the establishment and maintenance of diplomatic relations between South Korea and the nations of the world, while controlling for other factors that influence bilateral trading relations, we will demonstrate that having diplomatic relations is not simply a very important factor but perhaps the principal force behind what helps initiate trading relations between two nations and leads to increased volumes where trade relations already exist.[24] This will confirm findings in the scholarly literature such as those by Rose (2007) who showed that the establishment of an embassy led to trade increasing by 120 percent, and the creation of additional consular offices within a country increased bilateral trade by 6 percent to 10 percent for each office established.[25] More important than this, however, is that by demonstrating the positive impact of diplomacy on trade, we provide crucial evidence that the diplomatic efforts of South Korea's leaders were an important element of its domestic economic development strategy that helped put the country on the path to international influence long before it became the prosperous nation it is today.

What this means is that South Korea's diplomatic efforts are the key to understanding how it rose to international influence and became the important middle power it is today. Our efforts to make this connection will involve showing how such South Korean leaders as Park Chung-Hee, as well as those that followed, used diplomacy to promote the development and expansion of exports as a crucial element of the country's economic development strategy. They also sought expanded diplomatic connections simply as an effort to reconnect an internationally isolated South Korea with the rest of the world. Again, the Korean War left South Korea a poor, isolated, and utterly dependent nation, which meant that ending its isolation by rebuilding its international connections was a prerequisite for gaining international legitimacy and implementing an export-led domestic economic development strategy. Consequently, the diplomatic efforts of post-armistice leaders to establish formal relations with selected nations was a necessary first step in putting South Korea on the path to prosperity and international influence.

EXPLAINING SOUTH KOREA'S INTERNATIONAL RISE

We employ the "trade follows the flag" perspective to connect the diplomatic efforts of South Korea's leaders to trade expansion, domestic economic development, and, ultimately, to South Korea's rise to international influence because it offers us the most effective theoretical perspective to organize our overall political economy argument and to integrate the various components of the explanation we provide for South Korea's transformation into the prosperous and internationally influential middle power it has become. This theoretical perspective assists us by offering a way to tie together the efforts of South Korea's leaders to reconnect with the world and remove the country from international isolation and develop their country's economy by expanding its trading relations, thus enabling the implementation of the export-led development strategy that ultimately led to its growing prosperity. In light of this, the international goals set by South Korea's leaders become the first element of our explanation, which we discuss in terms of the succeeding presidential administrations that ruled the country throughout the post-armistice period.

Specifically, South Korea was led by thirteen presidents from the end of the Korean War to the present, and each presidential administration set different international goals with respect to the country's standing in the international economy and global politics. In addition to this, South Korea's presidents used different strategies to attain the goals they set because of the different international conditions they faced and the political and economic resources that they had available. Examples of such differences concern presidents' approaches to the communist world, and other parts of the world for that matter, as well as the fact that some presidents were more diplomatically aggressive than others while other presidents used different approaches to achieving the international goals they set as foreign policy targets. Specific illustrations that make this point include the contrasting approaches to relations with Japan followed by South Korea's first post-armistice president, Rhee Syngman, compared to General Park Chung-Hee, where the former followed a completely anti-Japan path while the latter was more open to reconciliation and engagement with Japan. Another illustration concerns the more open approach to North Korea taken by Presidents Kim Dae-Jung and Roh Moo-Hyun compared to all other South Korean Presidents, the fact that they were not monolithic in their approach notwithstanding.[26]

Most discussions of the international behavior of South Korea's presidents can be found in thematic articles published in Asia-related journals, and in the annual surveys of developments in individual Asian countries contained in the journal, *Asian Survey*.[27] This thematic literature sometimes covers the administration of a single president for a specific period of time, as do the survey articles in *Asian Survey*, and this is also true for the more extended treatment of the presidency of Lee Myung-Bak in Ikenberry and Mo (2013) and Park Guen-Hye in Sohn (2015), who focused on this administration in the context of South Korea as a new middle power.

To understand the goals that were set and the actions that were taken by South Korea's presidents, we must consider another factor, namely the different international conditions that these presidents faced throughout the post-armistice period. The importance of international conditions begins with the fact that the 1953 Armistice left Korea a divided nation, which is important because it required leaders in Seoul to conduct the nation's foreign relations in competition with a hostile regime in the North. Competition from Pyongyang added a level of urgency to South Korea's presidents to reestablish relations with countries with which it was formerly connected and with nations with which it did not previously have formal ties. This is especially true given that the early post-armistice period witnessed a rise in the number of new nations as more countries won their independence from colonial powers. It is also true because of the growing importance of the United Nations in adjudicating the reunification of the Korean Peninsula.

The United Nations became involved in helping a divided Korea through the United Nations Commission for the Unification and Rehabilitation of Korea (UNCURK). This was the specific international body that would decide how the division of the Korean Peninsula might be adjudicated and ultimately resolved, and its central role in this process meant that the support of member countries in the United Nations was paramount, leading Pyongyang and Seoul to establish formal ties with as many nations as they could. As a result, both countries began slowly changing their strategies by beginning to pursue foreign policies that courted the diplomatic favor of nations not formally part of their respective Cold War camps as well as the growing number of countries that joined the increasingly important movement of nonaligned nations.

With specific reference to South Korea's international ascendance, it was not simply the strategy of its leaders that led to its international rise nor was it the country's increasing prosperity that accounted for the dramatic transformation it experienced in the post-armistice period. Clearly, the international strategies implemented by South Korea's leaders as well as the increased diplomatic wherewithal provided by its rapid economic development were no doubt important factors. However, South Korea's leaders had placed it on the path to international prominence long before its rapid economic development allowed leaders to use their growing economic resources to achieve their international goals. Thus, the point here is that leadership strategy and economic resources worked hand in hand, and what molds this interaction is the opportunities and constraints presented to leaders by international conditions. Consequently, a complete explanation of South Korea's international transformation will require all three factors.

Now that we have summarized the problem we will address and how the "trade follows the flag" perspective integrates the components of our explanation for how South Korea transformed itself and became the influential middle power it is today, we turn to a summary of how we will accomplish the goals we have set out above. This will involve completing a number of tasks and the first involves us setting out and mapping the diplomatic contacts that South Korea's leaders were able to establish during their respective tenures as the country's chief executives. As part of this task, we must also provide an explanation for the country's diplomatic successes that we map, and then we must demonstrate that it was these diplomatic contacts that South Korea's leaders were able to establish that led to the great expansion of international trade it experienced, especially in the Cold War period. After completing these tasks, we then turn to how it was a combination of the diplomatic successes of South Korea's leaders and then the trade expansions and economic growth they encouraged that contribute to the explanation of how South Korea achieved the rise in international influence it achieved in the post-armistice period.

NOTES

1. Again, on the definition and significance of being a middle power, see e.g., Alexandroff and Cooper (2010) and Cooper and Flemes (2013). On South Korea as a middle power, see e.g., Lee (2012).

2. As we discuss in more detail below, the same cannot be said for the small number of scholarly works are complete and investigated both the diplomatic and economic aspects of South Korea's post-armistice rise in both the Cold War and post-Cold War periods.

3. Among the most important treatments here are Cummings (1997) and Ku (2018).

4. See e.g., Kim (1975) and Cummings (1997).

5. See e.g., Fuqua (2011) on Korean Unification, Kihl and Hayes (1997) and Rozman (2003) on the nuclear aspect of Inter-Korean relations, and Foley (2003) on divided families. Also, see Park and Snyder (2013) for the topic of economic cooperation in inter-Korea relations.

6. See Woo (2018) for a discussion of North Korean ideology. Also, for an excellent overall treatment of North Korea, see Cha (2012). See also the annual issues of the academic journal, *Asian Survey*, which include an annual discussion of political, economic, and international developments in North Korea.

7. See e.g., Park and Snyder (2013) for a recent collection of insightful essays on North Korean behavior and other topics.

8. See e.g., Giles (1996) and Newnham (2002).

9. For a discussion of the Nonaligned Movement and its importance for international politics during the Cold War, see Miskovic et. al., (2014).

10. For example, on South Korea's relations with the United States, see Lee (2006) and on South Korea's relationship with Japan, see Cha (1999).

11. It was not until 1965 that Japan and South Korea negotiated a formal end to their hostilities, and their bilateral relations have remained challenged since that time. See Cha (1999).

12. See Ku (2018) who divides the post-Armistice period into three phases for the purposes of discussing South Korean diplomacy. According to the discussion, in each succeeding phase, South Korean diplomacy became more independent of the United States.

13. For a discussion of South Korea's establishment of diplomatic relations with the Soviet Union, see e.g., Kim (1997).

14. They were also important, as we discuss in more detail below, because many of these nations formed trading relations with South Korea early on.

15. See Heo and Roehrig (2014) especially chapter 2.

16. For example, perhaps South Korea's most notable foreign policy change was with respect to its approach to North Korea, that is, the contrast of the Sunshine Policy of Kim Dae-Jung and his successor Roh Moo-Hyun compared to those who preceded and succeeded these presidents. However, this significant foreign policy change was far more a product of ideological and political differences of these presidents' political parties than economic development.

17. The "Miracle on the Han" refers to the Han River which flows through Seoul and has become a symbol of The ROK's rise to a position of international economic strength.

18. The concepts of open- and closed-access social orders in more fully developed in North, Wallis, and Weingast (2009).

19. There are a number of other scholarly works that have provided explanations for South Korea's economic transformation. See Jones and Sakong (1980) and Woo (1991) for treatments that emphasize the role played by the state and bureaucracy in this process. For a discussion of the role played by the South Korean military in the country's post-armistice economic development, see Kang (2002).

20. Rose (2007) includes relevant statements from the foreign offices of Canada, the United Kingdom, Germany, and Australia.

21. Ferguson and Forslid (2014) showed establishing an embassy led to a 5 percent increase in exports for Swedish firms. Lederman, Olarraga, and Payton (2010) revealed similar export increases given the efforts of export promotion agencies, and Nitsch (2007) showed that exports increased when there were official state visits.

22. An example here would be the French language and trade between France and its former African colonies.

23. There are many other currency unions such as that defined by the East Caribbean Dollar and two Franc-based currency unions, one in West Africa and the other in the South Pacific.

24. Again, past research has shown this to be true for nations in general. Again, see, Pollins (1989a and 1989b).

25. Rose (2007) used data averaged over 2002 and 2003 for twenty-two exporting nations the two hundred importing nations.

26. This is also true of South Korea's current president, Moon Jae-In.

27. A sampling of the journals referred to here are *Korea Observer, Pacific Focus, Pacific Affairs*, the *International Journal of Korean Studies.*

Chapter Three

Cold War Diplomacy and the Origins of South Korea's International Rise

The Division of the Korean Peninsula at the 38th parallel stands as a constant reminder that, even though we refer to the state of international affairs since 1989 as the post-Cold War world, Asian international relations is still defined by Cold-War conflicts. These include the dispute between Russia and Japan over the Northern Territories, the sovereignty dispute between China and Taiwan, and, most importantly for our purposes, the division of the Korean Peninsula into two sovereign states, the Democratic People's Republic of North Korea and the Republic of Korea. To be sure, scholars from different disciplines have analyzed these individual conflicts, and these scholarly efforts have defined the bases of each conflict, how they have evolved over time, their impacts on Asian international relations, and their respective likelihoods for resolution.

Specific studies of these conflicts as well as the overall scholarly literature on international relations during the Cold War and post-Cold War periods have been informative to be sure, but there is a curious aspect to the analyses we have of the international divisions that existed in interstate relations and among the states of East Asia in particular. Virtually all scholarly efforts to understand the international relations of the Cold War period have not simply focused on East and West Europe and the patterns that defined interstate relations on that continent but rather used the Cold War in Europe to inform international relations around the world. This European emphasis in Cold War perspectives led scholars to take the strict bipolarity that defined European relations, and the United States's and Soviet Union's immediate spheres of influence, and impose it on the entire globe as an organizing concept for all international relations of this period.[1] While there was clearly a logic to this bipolarity understanding of global international relations during the Cold War, assumptions that the bipolarity of the world system applied equally to all regions of the globe proved to be untenable, especially with respect to interstate relations in Asia.

Bipolarity during the Cold War was due to the fact that world politics was divided into two camps with a superpower at the head of each camp, the United States and the Soviet Union. Given that an open conflict between these two nuclear powers would most likely have led to the destruction of the world, they were naturally cautious in how they approached potential conflicts with each other.[2] This situation was noted by scholars who then interpreted the bipolar international relations of the Cold War period as being inherently more stable and predictable than the preceding balance of power period of World War I and II.[3] Unfortunately, international relations in Asia have manifested a somewhat different dynamic that involved interstate relations there being much more conflict prone. Consequently, in contrast to the relative stability of Cold War Europe, East and Southeast Asia have the reputation of being the place where the Cold War turned hot, and not once but two times.

The first instance of the Cold War turning hot was the Korean War when North Korean forces crossed the 38th parallel and attempted to unify the Korean Peninsula by force.[4] Korea had been a unified country for its entire history, and this tragic division occurred not just because the forces of the U.S. and the Soviet Union occupied two different regions of the Peninsula after the Japanese surrendered, and not just because the world's major powers could not agree on a format for the reunification of the Peninsula, either among themselves or through the United Nations. The Korean Peninsula remains divided also because, in the immediate aftermath of the Japanese surrender, the will of Korea's leaders and people was largely ignored by the great powers,[5] which allowed competing regimes in the northern and southern parts of the peninsula to be set up and established for the long term.

The failure of international politics to solve the problem of a divided Korea weighed heavily on the minds of South Korea's leaders and helped motivate them to take action to remove their nation from the dependence and isolation from which it suffered in the aftermath of the Korean War.[6] Indeed, the conditions that South Korea's leaders faced in the early post-armistice period were such that this nation was at an extreme disadvantage in terms of its international position. South Korea was a very poor nation to begin with, and the Japanese occupation helped maintain the South's poverty because it promoted an unequal distribution of industrial resources between the Northern and Southern parts of the peninsula. This means that the little industry that South Korea did possess was destroyed by the North's invasion. Moreover, South Korea emerged from the Korean War facing significant constraints in its international behavior because of the strict power hierarchies and alliance rigidities that defined the Cold War years. The dominance of the United States and the Soviet Union allowed for little diplomatic flexibility on the part of NATO and Warsaw Pact bloc member states, and the dependence of the South Korean economy and government on the U.S. for financial assistance and security made it initially very difficult for South Korea's leaders to pursue policies that would help grow the country's prosperity.

Despite the immense international constraints and domestic challenges its leaders faced, it is in the Cold War period that South Korea's leaders overcame the inauspicious conditions they faced and put the country on the path to prosperity and international influence. Evidence for this, as we will show in the following two chapters, is witnessed in how South Korea's Cold War presidents implemented domestic policies that encouraged rapid and ongoing economic growth. More importantly, these same leaders established diplomatic connections that not simply helped rebuild South Korea's international legitimacy and remove it from the international isolation it experienced in the immediate post-armistice years, but more importantly allowed it to start trading relations with more and more countries so that its export-led development strategy could be implemented and lead to the levels of economic development its leaders desired.

This was no easy task for South Korea's leaders as they not only had to overcome the international constraints of the Cold War period, they more importantly had to pursue their goals in the context of the Korean Peninsula's version of the Hallstein Doctrine, which prohibited countries from establishing diplomatic relations with the Republic of Korea if they already established relations with its rival, North Korea. This added a sense of urgency to the diplomatic efforts of South Korea's leaders, who registered numerous diplomatic successes in spite of this constraint. Among these successes included the building of extensive diplomatic relations not just with nations friendly to the non-communists allies of the United States but also with nations on the other side of the Cold War divide. As part of these diplomatic achievements, South Korean leaders succeeded in laying the groundwork to realizing the goals of its export-led economic development strategy and ultimately paving the way for it to become an internationally influential middle power, possessing memberships in numerous international organizations.

COLD WAR DIPLOMACY

As stated above, South Korea emerged from the armistice that ended the Korean War as a poor and divided nation that was utterly dependent on the United States for its economic survival as well as its security in a region that remained prone to conflict. The international conditions that South Korea's leaders faced were limiting to be sure, and when combined with it being devastated by the war and in a state of extreme poverty, its potential to overcome these negatives appeared dim. Despite such inauspicious beginnings, South Korea transformed itself, and the reasons for this rest on the fact that, with aid from the United States and then Japan, South Korea's presidents set specific domestic and international goals and pursued a variety of different strategies to achieve these goals. The result was South Korea's leaders placing the country squarely on the path to the prosperity and international prominence that it currently possesses, Cold War constraints notwithstanding.

When we say that one set of goals was international, we are referring to the diplomatic goals that South Korean presidents set during these Cold War years and to the strategies they derived and implemented to achieve these goals. In this process, our purpose is to demonstrate how it was during these Cold War years, when the country was still poor, that its leaders raised its international status and put the country on the path that led ultimately to this once poor and isolated nation becoming the prosperous and internationally influential actor it is today. We will accomplish this by mapping the diplomatic connections South Korea's leaders established during this period and then assessing the international successes and setbacks the country experienced throughout the period of the Cold War.

At the present time, South Korea has diplomatic relations with over 180 nations and is an influential member of numerous international organizations. Examples of such achievements include South Korea's leaders being able to secure a membership on the Executive Board of the International Monetary Fund (IMF) and on the Development Assistance Committee (DAC) of the Organization for Economic Cooperation and Development (OECD). Moreover, South Korea was very influential in developing the trajectory of the G20 and even witnessed one of its former Foreign Ministers serving as United Nations Secretary General.[7] As a number of scholars have written, it is clear that its rise to international prominence accelerated in the last two to three decades because, by this time, South Korea had achieved a level of economic development sufficient for it to employ such resources in service of its goal to become the influential middle power it is today.[8] On the other hand, we need to emphasize here that these more recent developments would not have resulted in the great influence that South Korea now possesses were it not for the international achievements its leaders accomplished during the Cold War years. This is important because South Korea's diplomatic achievements during the Cold War years were accomplished before it became the developed and prosperous nation it is today.[9]

The diplomatic connections established by South Korea's leaders during the Cold War period are contained in Table 3.1. They are broken down by this period's presidential administrations which begin with the first post-independence president, Rhee Syngman, and they end with the country's transition president of Roh Tae-Woo, who continued to rule the nation after the Cold War in Europe ended. Among other things, the six presidents who led South Korea during the Cold War were characterized by varying lengths of time in office and very different levels of success at establishing formal diplomatic relations with other nations. As we see from the data in the table, the length of time a president held office does help explain the level of diplomatic success he enjoyed, but there were certainly other factors at work as well. In terms of length of time in office, the shortest terms were held by Yun Bo-Sun and Choi Gyu-Ha, each of whom did not manage to establish any new formal relations between South Korea and another nation.[10] The longest term was held by Park Chung-Hee who established the most formal diplomatic connections throughout the Cold War years.[11]

Table 3.1. Diplomatic Successes of Korea's Presidents in the Pre- and Post-Transition Periods

Presidents/ Dates in Office	*Embassies*	*Consuls*	*Representatives*	*Total*
Rhee Syngman 1948–1960	9	4	2	15
Yun Bosun 1960–1961	0	0	0	0
Park Chunghee 1961–1979	55	20	0	77
Choi Gyuha 1979–1980	0	0	0	0
Chun Doowhan 1980–1988	17	4	1	22
Roh Taewoo 1988–1993	8	3	1	12

Source: Compiled by the authors from COW Diplomatic Exchange Data v. 2006.

President Park Chung-Hee was followed in length of term by Chun Doo-Hwan (nine years) and Roh Tae-Woo (six years), who established twenty-two and twelve formal diplomatic connections respectively, making them the second and third-most diplomatically successful among South Korean presidents. Their terms in office confirm that a president's length of time in office is directly related to that chief executive's diplomatic success as a president of South Korea. However, the Chun and Roh presidencies both provide excellent illustrations of how other factors were also important in determining the diplomatic successes of a South Korean leader. While President Chun was responsible for establishing diplomatic relations with such Asian nations as Bhutan, Pakistan, Brunei, and Macao, he also was successful in placing South Korean embassies in such African nations as Somalia, Nigeria, Libya, and Guinea-Bisseau. Moreover, his presidency set the stage for the diplomatic successes that his successor, Roh Tae-Woo, would have, especially with respect the nations that had been under the suzerainty of the former Soviet Union.

As alluded to above, what is important about the diplomatic successes of Chun Doo-Hwan in particular is that they illustrate the importance of how the process of establishing and maintaining formal diplomatic relations is influenced by factors other than simply the time a president spent in office. These factors involve both domestic and international influences and how these two sets of factors often interact with each other. In the case of Chun Doo-Hwan, the Berlin Wall was still operating as a barrier between Eastern and Western Europe, which meant that the number of nations available for South Korea to connect with had declined with the diplomatic successes of his predecessors. This is very different from the international environment his successor, Roh Tae-Woo, faced because he had a growing number of former Soviet allied states available for the establishment of formal diplomatic relations. Moreover, President Chun ascended to South Korea's chief executive position through a military coup, and he followed his taking the presidency with the brutal repression of movements that opposed his taking the presidency. This was particularly true of the opposition movements that took place in Gwangju in Southern Cholla Province, which he brutally repressed and which culminated in numerous deaths.[12] This tragic event and his repressive political style, which included threatening opposition leader Kim Dae-Jung with death, led to worsened relations with South Korea's allies. This was true at least initially for the United States where relations had worsened under President Jimmy Carter but improved with Ronald Reagan taking office, and it was also true of relations with Japan which threatened to cut off aid if any harm came to Kim Dae-Jung. While President Chun then had to utilize his country's diplomatic resources to improve relations with these important allies, he also had to deal with an assassination attempt in Yangon, Myanmar, where an explosion killed a number of South Korean officials. Moreover, he was also consumed by a crisis that was caused by the Soviet Union destroying a Korean Air Line passenger jet in the infamous KAL 007 incident.

Despite such variation across the presidencies of the Cold War years, the data in Figure 3.1 confirm our point that the leaders of South Korea during this time were very successful at reconnecting their nation to the world. The magnitude of South Korea's diplomatic successes should not be understated because, as discussed above, of the severe international constraints the nation faced throughout this period, especially in both the early and later years of the Cold War. They should also be recognized for their significance for one other reason, specifically, the fact that, throughout this time, South Korea was not the prosperous nation that it is today. During the Cold War, South Korea was

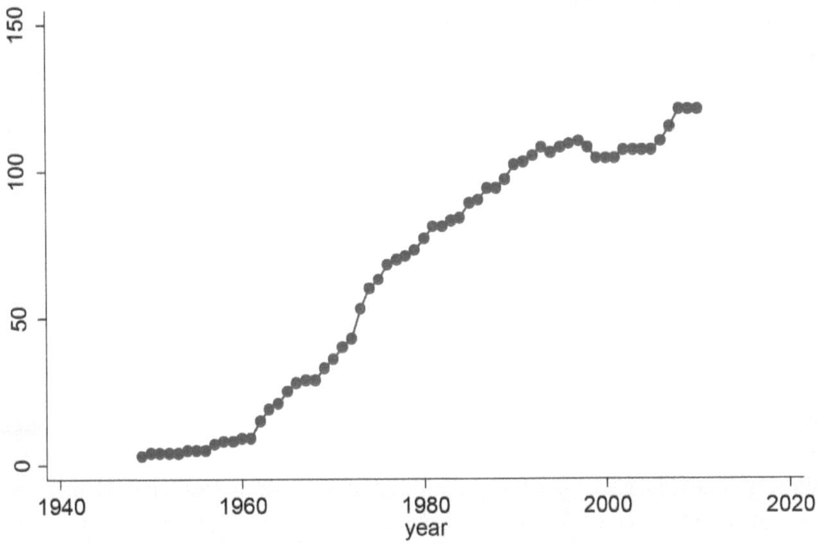

Figure 3.1. South Korean Embassies.

a relatively poor nation; nonetheless, as its leaders successfully reestablished its connections with the nations of the world, they also began ensuring that it was on the path to its international rise. This point is confirmed by the data in Table 3.2.

Table 3.2. Embassy Establishment and Per Capita GDP in South Korea During the Cold War

Presidents/Dates in Office	*Percentage of All Embassies Established During Presidential Tenure*	*Year and Per Capita GDP*
Rhee Syngman and Yun Bosun 1948–1961	10.1%	1960 / $158.24
Park Chunghee 1961–1979	61.8%	1961 / $98.32 1979 / $1,773.47
Choi Gyuha 1979–1980	0.0%	1980 / $1,704.47
Chun Doowhan 1980–1988	19.1%	1981 / $1,870.34 1988 / $4,686.14
Roh Taewoo 1988–1993	9.0%	1989 / $5,736.90 1993 / $8,740.95

Source: Compiled by the authors from COW Diplomatic Exchange Data (2006) and the World Bank.

This is undoubtedly true for the period that Rhee Syngman was president as he was responsible for establishing 10 percent of the formal diplomatic connections that South Korea managed to establish in the early post-armistice period. We see from the data that South Korea's per capita GDP in 1960, the year that President Rhee was forced from office, was $158.24, a level just above that of the country of Bolivia. However, we also see from the table that it was true for the nearly twenty years that Park Chung-Hee ruled the country. This is important because President Park is the leader responsible for implementing South Korea's export-led economic development strategy and putting the country on the path to prosperity. What is not well known is that it was President Park Chung-Hee who was responsible for over 60 percent of the formal diplomatic connections that South Korea's Cold War leaders were able to establish.

What is important about President Park's diplomatic success is that, throughout the 1960s, South Korea's per capita GDP averaged $200, an amount that was actually behind the GDP of Bolivia and other Andean countries at the time. Over the next decade, South Korea's per capita GDP more than doubled, but it increased only to $500 per capita, again indicating that the nation remained a member of the family of poorer nations. In fact, the data in the figure indicate that, when Park Chung-Hee was assassinated in 1979, South Korea's per capita GDP was $1,773.53. This was substantially higher than when the military coup placed Park in power, and it tells us that Park's efforts were successful because South Korea's GDP had pulled ahead of Bolivia's by over $900. Nonetheless, it was still behind other relatively poor nations like Ecuador.

What the data in Table 3.2 also tell us is how growth in South Korea's per capita GDP accelerated throughout the remainder of the Cold War period. In fact, when the Berlin Wall came down in 1989, South Korea's per capita GDP had grown to nearly $6,000. This amount was well beyond the GDPs of all South American nations, which attests to how economically successful South Korea had become. Indeed, it was during these years that its economic development policies began to bear fruit, but its road to prosperity was paved with its leaders' diplomatic efforts during this period, and we turn next to how South Korea's leaders successfully reconnected it to the world.

KOREA'S EARLY DIPLOMATIC CONNECTIONS

Korea's earliest diplomatic connections rested on the long period of political and economic engagements it maintained with many of its neighbors in the Northeast Asian region.[13] As Kang (2010) notes, these interactions were made formal in the early fifteenth century when the Korean Court during the Chosun Dynasty was placed firmly in the orbit of the Sinocentric tribute system that governed international relations in Asia from the late 1400s. This means that initially Korea's most important diplomatic contact at this time was with China's Ming Dynasty. This connection began in 1393, and, at the same time, Korea sent envoys to and received officials from other nations that were part of this Asian tribute system. Most important among these nations were the Ryukyus, Japan, and the Jurchens,[14] all of which were part of system of interstate relations that persisted for centuries. Indeed, this Asian tribute system continued until the arrival of the Europeans undermined the power and influence of China and ultimately replaced this system with the imperialist colonial arrangement that eventually led to South Korea losing its sovereignty when it was annexed by Japan in 1910.

Throughout the multiple centuries that it was a part of the Sinocentric tribute system, Korea was a unified country whose leaders pursued its foreign relations in obeisance to certain international imperatives. These imperatives can be captured in what have become the enduring themes of Korea's history, which most notably are defined by the country's struggles to preserve its unique cultural and linguistic identity while, at the same time, maintaining its national sovereignty and political independence. These struggles trace their genesis to and have been sustained by Korea's unique geography of being situated between two large and powerful neighbors, China and Japan.

Korea's geography has certainly influenced its international relations and not just between itself and China and Japan. The realities of Korean geography and history have also involved relations between these two large neighbors themselves, which at times profoundly affected the ability of Korea's leaders to maintain the country's independence and protect its cultural uniqueness. This is because leaders in China and Japan have long viewed control of Korea as a necessary step to protect their own country's sovereignty from the other.[15] In fact, as Gu (1995) has noted, Koreans have captured this geographic and historical theme by using a simile to describe their country's position in the Northeast Asian region. Specifically, Koreans liken their country to a "shrimp among whales."[16]

Despite its challenging geographic position, Korea's leaders were able to secure their country's sovereignty from the fourteenth to the seventeenth centuries. They accomplished this by securing a loosely integrated but subordinate position in the hierarchical Asian tribute system. In this position, as long as the Korean Court paid its tribute to the Chinese Emperor, its territorial integrity was guaranteed by the Chinese military, and, at this time, China's protection of Korean sovereignty even allowed it to enjoy a modest degree of flexibility in its international behavior. However, in the seventeenth century, the price for Korea's security was increased as this flexibility was diminished when Chinese leaders required that Korea be fully integrated into its Sino-centric tribute system. To be sure, this resulted in the enhanced protection of Korea's borders, but it also diminished Korea's sovereignty because the Chinese allowed the Japanese to maintain a trading post in Korea's southernmost port city of Busan.[17]

Despite this intrusion on Korean sovereignty, the security of the country was still maintained under this hierarchical Asian Tribute system, at least until the late eighteenth and early nineteenth centuries. It was at this time that imperialist powers from Europe and the United States increasingly encroached on the sovereignty of Japan and China. Imperialist challenges against China threatened that nation's very territorial integrity, which over time rendered it less and less able to serve credibly as the dominant power of the tribute-based international system it led. As a result, it was less and less able to protect itself let alone its vassal state of Korea. Japan's sovereignty was also subjected to similar imperialist encroachments, but instead of following China's path of denial, combined with token resistance, Japanese leaders allowed their country's sovereignty to be compromised under the unequal treaty system. In following this path, however, Japan's leaders enacted policies that swept away all remnants of its erstwhile traditional society and government and commenced building a modern nation state that would ultimately free itself from the unequal treaty system imposed on it by Western imperialists.

What is important about the efforts of Japanese leaders at this time is not simply that they ultimately succeeded in transforming their country into a modern nation state but, more importantly, that they put Japan on a course where it behaved more and more like the Western imperialists that forced it to end its isolation and, ultimately, ended the tribute system of international relations that existed for five centuries.[18] Japan's increasingly imperialistic behavior was encouraged by the regional power vacuum left by an increasingly subjugated China, and it resulted in growing pressure on Korea which, as stated briefly above, China was less and less able to protect. Japan's encroachments on Korea reached an initial high point in 1876 after Koreans attacked a Japanese naval vessel in an effort to protect their country's isolation. Japan sent its fleet in response and pressured Korea into signing a treaty of commerce, ending its status as a vassal state of China and formally establishing it as an independent nation.

With Korea being independent from China, it began receiving diplomatic missions and establishing its own foreign offices abroad. It was at this time in the late 1880s that Korea first appears in the Correlates of War Diplomatic Exchange Data,[19] and, from its first appearance until the beginning of the twentieth century, it was in the bottom five of nations sending and receiving diplomatic and consular officials.[20] Its ranking was just below those of Colombia, Siam, and Morocco, but just above those of Haiti and the Dominican Republic. This ranking in the Correlates of War Diplomatic Exchange Data did change somewhat over the next few years as Korea moved up a few positions but still remained in the bottom ten of nations sending and receiving diplomatic missions among sovereign, independent nations. While this upward movement in Korea's diplomatic status may have continued, it disappears from the diplomatic exchange data after 1910. This is because Korea lost its independence when it was absorbed as a colony in Japan's expanding colonial empire.

Japan's colonization of Korea lasted until August of 1945, when Tokyo accepted the terms of the Potsdam Declaration and agreed to an unconditional surrender. While Japan's surrender ended its colonization of Korea, it did not result in Korea regaining its sovereignty right away.[21] In the immediate aftermath of Japan's surrender, South Korea was ruled by the United States through a military government, which continued until August 1948 after which Korea became an independent republic. Thus, it was not until this time that the Republic of Korea once again began to establish diplomatic relations with selected nations, even though these efforts were cut short by the invasion of North Korea in June 1950.[22] This war ended three years later in a stalemate that was enshrined in the Armistice of 1953. This armistice did not lead to a reunification of the country, and, as a result, Korea was forced to enter the Cold War as a sovereign but divided nation.

SOUTH KOREAN DIPLOMACY DURING THE COLD WAR

When the armistice that ended hostilities on the Korean Peninsula was negotiated, South Korea was not just poor and ravaged from the destruction of the North's invasion: it was also dependent on the United States for both its economic wellbeing and for its security protection. At the same time, South Korea was internationally isolated, having formal diplomatic relations with very few nations. The Correlates of War Diplomatic Exchange data revealed that South Korea had fewer than five formal diplomatic connections when the Korean War ended, and, until 1960, its formal diplomatic connections remained fewer than fifteen.[23] In addition to this, when the armistice ending the war on the Korean Peninsula was promulgated, South Korea ranked dead last in this data set's measures of diplomatic importance.[24]

Korea's division reflected the Cold War world that was sectioned off into Western (NATO) and Communist (Warsaw Pact) camps, and while these divisions meant that South Korea was left with little diplomatic flexibility, its leaders managed to overcome these constraints throughout the Cold War years and elevate its place in the world. The data presented in Figure 3.1 are a count of the number of embassies and consulates South Korea formally established in various nations throughout the world.[25] As the data in the figure reveal, from 1955 to the end of that decade, South Korea more than doubled the number of embassies it established. At the same time, it sent a half dozen consuls abroad as well as two representatives to international organizations.

In the 1960s, Korea's diplomatic presence in the world grew even more dramatically than it did in the first years after the Korean War. Indeed, South Korea's leadership managed to almost triple the number of embassies it maintained in foreign capitals, and it also doubled the number of consuls it sent abroad. In addition to these achievements, the data in Figure 3.1 above indicate that growth in South Korea's formal diplomatic contacts continued to grow over the next two decades, albeit at a somewhat slower pace. By the end of the 1980s, when the Cold War had ended, South Korea maintained embassies in over one hundred nations, a growth of over 2000 percent from the time the armistice that ended the Korean War went into effect.

Another way to reveal how significant South Korea's diplomatic achievements were in the post-armistice period is to evaluate how they compare to similar efforts made by other nations, friend and foe alike. To make such a comparison, the Correlates of War Diplomatic Exchange data contain a measure they refer to as a country's international status. This measure is created as the ratio of the number of diplomatic connections a country has with the number of diplomatic connections established by the nation with the highest number of diplomatic missions in its capital.[26] Data capturing South Korea's changing international status are contained in Figure 3.2, and they indicate that the efforts of South Korea's leaders in the Cold War period paid off because the country's international status rose as leaders successfully established formal diplomatic connections with other nations. As we see from data in the figure, by 1960, South Korea had only 10 percent of the number of embassies in Seoul as did the United States. This changed dramatically over the next ten years as its ranking grew dramatically. The rate of increase in South Korea's diplomatic connections slowed in the mid- to late-1970s,[27] but the data in the figure tell us that Korea's international status continued to increase, reaching over 60 percent of the world's number one diplomatic power by end of the Cold War.

To be sure, this comparative measure of international status is important for indicating how successful South Korea's leaders were at removing the country from international isolation by creating formal diplomatic connections. However, there is one more comparison that perhaps reveals even more how diplomatically successful South Korea's presidents were during the Cold War. This comparison begins with the fact that the 1953 Armistice left Korea

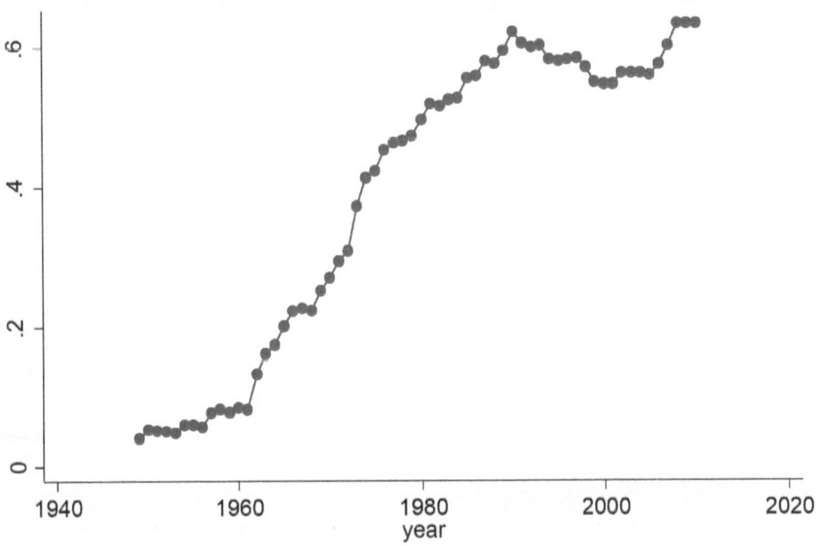

Figure 3.2. Changes in South Korea's International Status.

a divided nation, which is significant for our discussion because it required leaders in Seoul to conduct the nation's foreign relations in competition with a hostile North Korea. Competition from the North added a level of urgency to the efforts of South Korea's presidents to reestablish relations with countries with which it was formerly connected and with nations with which it did not have formal ties. This is especially true given that the early post-armistice period witnessed a rise in the number of new nations as more countries won their independence from colonial powers. It is also true because of the growing importance of the United Nations in adjudicating the reunification of the Korean Peninsula.

As mentioned briefly above, in the aftermath of the 1953 Armistice, both North and South Korea initially pursued their respective diplomatic efforts while adhering to the Peninsula's version of the Hallstein Doctrine. This meant that both North and South Korea claimed to be the only legitimate government on the Korean Peninsula, and, thus, any country establishing diplomatic relations with one could not then establish diplomatic relations with the other. Adherence to this doctrine led to a predictable pattern in the diplomatic efforts of North and South Korea in the early post-armistice years in that each initially sought connections with its set of core nations within the Soviet and NATO blocs. North Korea's initial diplomatic contacts were with nations in the Moscow and Beijing orbits, and South Korea's contacts were with nations allied with the United States.[28]

As time progressed, however, there were a growing number of nonaligned nations that were open to contacts from North and South Korea, and support from these nations would become increasingly important. This is because the problem of reunifying the Korean Peninsula was initially left to United Nations. Specifically, the United Nations Commission for the Unification and Rehabilitation of Korea (UNCURK) became the international body that would decide how the division of the Korean Peninsula might be adjudicated and ultimately resolved. This meant that the support of member countries in the United Nations was paramount, leading Pyongyang and Seoul to establish formal ties with as many nations as they could. As a result, both countries began pursuing foreign policies that courted the diplomatic favor of nations not formally part of their respective Cold War camps as well as the growing number of countries that joined the increasingly important movement of nonaligned nations. Such efforts would ultimately lead to both nations not adhering to the Hallstein Doctrine so they could establish a greater number of diplomatic connections than its competitor.

In a rather short time, the diplomatic efforts of North and South Korea would redound more to the benefit of the South than its competitor in the North. The data in Figure 3.3 compare the number of formal diplomatic connections established by both North and South Korea from the beginning of the

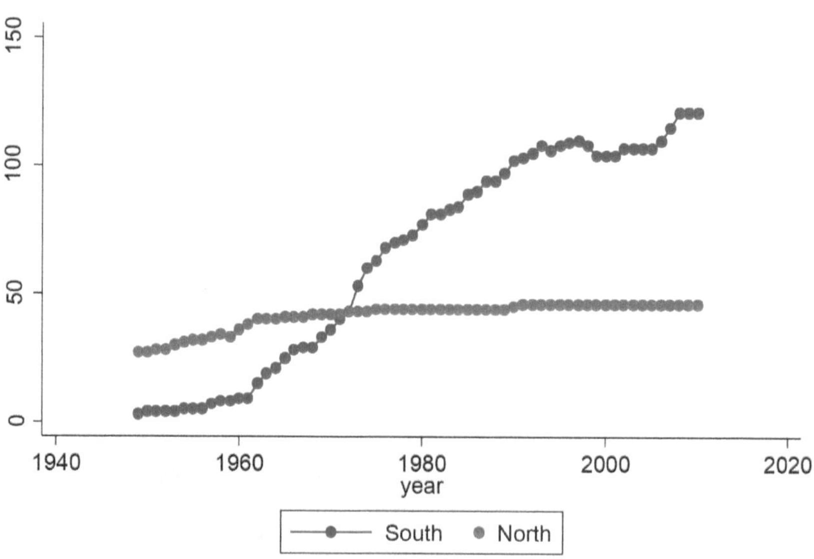

Figure 3.3. North Korean vs. South Korean Embassies.

post-armistice period to the present. The data are clear that, at the beginning of the post-armistice period, the North maintained a clear advantage over the South in terms of the number of formal diplomatic connections it successfully established. This is because both countries at the time were reliant principally on the nations that were committed to their respective blocs, as well as the rising number of nonaligned nations that were generally more sympathetic to the Soviet-aligned, socialist bloc. Until 1960, this advantage was not large, but it was solid. After Park Chung-Hee took power in 1961, however, this initial northern advantage declined rapidly and then disappeared by the early 1970s, when the number of South Korea's formal diplomatic connections exceeded those obtained by Pyongyang. The data in the figure indicate that, while the number of countries having diplomatic relations with North Korea leveled off, South Korea's numbers continued to grow at a fast, steady rate. This is true for the presidency of Chun Doo-Hwan, which was challenged with repairing relations with a number of allies, but it was also true for his successor, Roh Tae-Woo, who began building connections with many former allies of the Soviet Union.

When measured strictly as the number of formal diplomatic connections, we see that comparing the diplomatic efforts of leaders in Seoul and Pyongyang reveal the continued growth of South Korea's connections with those of the North increasing slightly early on but then remaining flat until the present day. When we change our measure to the international status of each country, the success of South Korea becomes even more notable. As the data in Figure 3.4 make clear, early in the post-armistice period, the international status of North Korea was significantly above that of its competitor in the South. This difference in status was even larger than we would expect given the comparatively smaller difference between the two with respect to the number of formal diplomatic connections. Moreover, from the early 1960s to the end of the Cold War, we see that the international status of South Korea increased rapidly while that of its rival in the North experienced a slight but nonetheless monotonic decline, which continues to the present day.

The international conditions that favored North Korea very early in the post-Armistice period centered on two characteristics of the new countries that were joining the family of nations at the time. First, many of these nations were developing nations, which is significant because their respective leaders found the models of development promoted by Moscow and Beijing more appealing than that of the United States and the West. This support was true more for the earlier years of the post-armistice period because, as the realities of the Soviet model were revealed, it lost support among developing nations. This weakening of support for the Soviet model of development was also encouraged by the development experience of such Asian nations

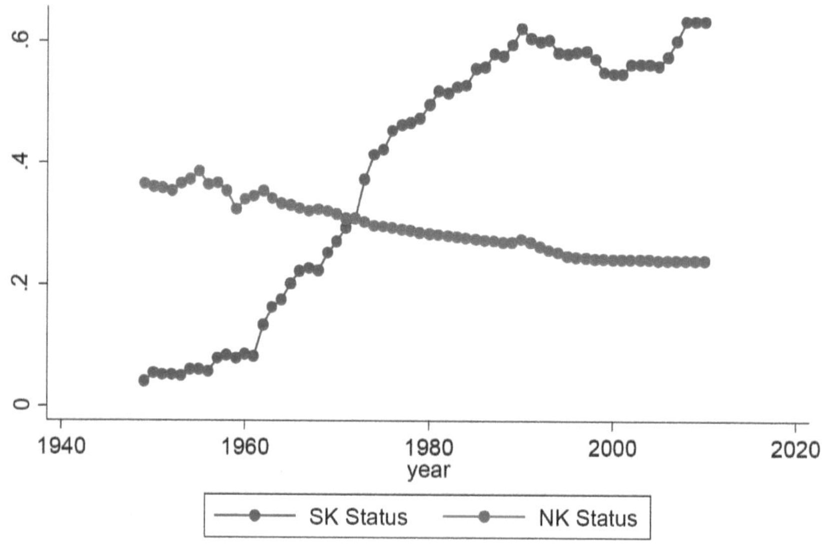

Figure 3.4. International Status Changes, North vs. South Korea.

as Japan, South Korea, and Taiwan when their economic progress indicated a more certain path to successful economic development. Nonetheless, until these developments were more widely understood, the early post-armistice period favored the North diplomatically.

The second characteristic of the new countries that joined the family of nations in the post-armistice period was that many were former colonies of European nations. These newly independent nations won back their sovereignty from the colonial powers that occupied them and ruled their respective populations for many years. The colonial powers that ruled these newly independent nations were by and large Western powers, current members of NATO, and, thus, generally allies of the United States. As a result, a majority of these newly independent nations were more sympathetic to the anticolonial and socialist programs represented by the Soviet Bloc of nations. With these and such other inducements as the Hallstein Doctrine, the initial predisposition of these former colonies then was to establish diplomatic relations with North Korea.

Despite these initial North Korean advantages, we see that leaders in the South quickly overcame the constraints they faced and increased their country's formal diplomatic connections while at the same time raising its international status. These dramatic changes raise the question of how South Korea's presidents were able to turn this situation around and put their country on the path to international influence. We turn to this topic in the next section, providing a more comprehensive explanation for South Korea's ability to remove itself from international isolation. In this explanation, we focus on two transitions that occurred in South Korea's approach to its relations with the nations of the world. The first of these concerns the political transition that occurred between the presidency of Rhee Syngman and General Park Chung-Hee, and the second concerns the response of the South Korean leadership to those international conditions that led ultimately to the abandonment of adherence to the Hallstein Doctrine.

TRANSITIONS AND SOUTH KOREA'S DIPLOMATIC SUCCESSES DURING THE COLD WAR

The American educated Rhee Syngman became president of the Republic of Korea when its first presidential election was held in 1948.[29] Rhee's presidency was undoubtedly tumultuous with respect to domestic politics, which contributed to his rule being reactionary and inconsistent. On the other hand, his approach to promoting the international interests of South Korea was very consistent, albeit not without growing disagreement from other members of the country's ruling elites and his country's most important ally, the United States. President Rhee had three goals that defined the foreign policy agenda he would implement as the Republic's first post-independence president. He formulated these goals after the armistice formally ended hostilities on the Korean Peninsula in 1953 but left the country divided and, over time, with diminishing hopes for a peaceful reunification at any time in the near future.

The first of these goals concerned South Korea's relations with the free world but most importantly with the United States. As mentioned above, South Korea was very dependent on the United States early in the post-armistice period. The extent of its dependence was such that South Korea ended up using U.S. facilities for some of its diplomatic missions, and the government in Seoul required U.S. financial assistance to cover the costs of programs in its National Budget.[30] This situation behooved President Rhee to be very attentive to relations with the United States, but it also made the United States's NATO allies priority nations for diplomatic connections with South Korea. In Europe, President Rhee moved to connect with the United States's non-communist allies, and the COW Diplomatic Exchange Data indicate that these nations included France, Spain, and the U.K. just before the outbreak of the Korean War and West Germany, Italy, Norway, Sweden, and Denmark when hostilities on the peninsula ended.

These West European nations were not the only ones with which President Rhee established formal diplomatic connections because he also pursued relations with certain nations in Asia, including the Philippines, Thailand, and Malaysia. Like his establishment of relations with the nations of West Europe, formal diplomatic relations were established with these Southeast Asian nations because they were noncommunist nations that were also former colonies of Japan. These nations were also allied with the United States, which gave them priority status for diplomatic relations with Rhee Syngman's South Korea.

The second goal of President Rhee's foreign policy rested on his extreme anti-Japan orientation, which led him to render avoidance of any formal relations with South Korea's former occupier a pillar of his country's foreign policy. Clearly, this was an emotional issue for the President as it was for most Koreans, but there was also a pragmatic side to Rhee's anti-Japan stance. Given that there were manifest differences at this time in Japan's versus South Korea's level of economic development, Rhee wanted to be certain that his country would never again be dominated by Japan, even in an economic sense. Consequently, to keep his country from being subjected to the second-class status it had experienced throughout the colonial period, President Rhee did not allow any formal political connections with Japan, either political or economic. Indeed, he made it clear that he would not allow the two nations to move toward rapprochement despite growing pressure from the United States.

The third goal of the foreign policy of Rhee Syngman was initially something with which he had the complete support of the United States, and the reference here is to his very strong policy of anti-communism. Naturally, the United States's confrontation with the communist Soviet Union and, after 1949, the People's Republic of China, made Rhee a natural and important ally, especially after the Korean War made it clear that communist nations were not averse to using military force to accomplish their expansionist goals. Rhee's anti-communism also made his South Korea a natural ally of the non-communist nations of Southeast Asia and elsewhere. However, despite South Korea and the United States sharing an anti-communist vision, there were aspects of Rhee's approach that made U.S. officials increasingly uncomfortable and even concerned that the Rhee presidency might promote instability and undermine U.S. interests in the Northeast Asian region.

One of these concerned Rhee's increasingly hostile approach to the North and his propensity to repress any opposition to his anti-North Korea stance at home. While the Armistice of 1953 ended formal military hostilities on the peninsula, no peace treaty was negotiated and promulgated between the two nations. As a result, a formal state of war existed between Pyongyang and

Seoul, which helped render any challenge to the authority of President Rhee's administration interpretable as an act in favor of the communist North. Rhee's domestic political repression combined with the growing impression that he was wont to take military action to unify the peninsula, led to his becoming more unpopular with his U.S. ally.

This was not the only reason that U.S. officials experienced growing concerns over the Rhee Administration, and perhaps next in importance concerned the large amount of economic aid the United States was providing despite its increasingly expensive Cold War commitments. It was not simply that South Korea was solely dependent on the United States for economic aid and that the United States wanted to reduce amounts it extended to Seoul, given the growing costs of its own international burdens. Rather, it was also how President Rhee dispensed with the extensive amount of economic aid his country received from the United States. Specifically, U.S. officials became increasingly concerned that President Rhee was diverting larger shares of the resources he received to purchase consumption goods and, more importantly, to shore up his domestic support levels, which had been sagging because of his repressive practices. U.S. officials also witnessed rampant corruption in the Rhee government to be sure, but the problem was also what they did not see from the administration of President Rhee. Specifically, U.S. officials did not see any well thought out plan whereby U.S. aid would be utilized to help develop the South Korean economy.[31]

As we see from the data in Table 3.3, in 1960, 99 percent of the economic aid South Korea received was from the United States. Because of its growing Cold War burdens, the United States wanted Japan to assume a greater share of the burden for providing economic aid to South Korea. In 1960, Japan provided nothing to South Korea, and Rhee's anti-Japan position would see that it remained at this level. As stated briefly above, the Cold War continued to increase the international burdens of the United States, and this rendered

Table 3.3. Sources of Economic Aid Received by South Korea, 1960-1995

	U.S.	*Japan*	*Others**
1960	99.32%	0.00%	0.68%
1965	73.13%	22.39%	4.48%
1970	56.17%	38.86%	4.98%
1975	39.56%	34.10%	26.34%
1980	22.48%	60.08%	17.43%
1985	6.03%	72.83%	21.14%
1990	1.36%	81.67%	16.97%
1995	0.00%	87.43%	12.57%

* Includes economic aid from multilateral sources
Source: compiled by the authors from OECD ODA data.

South Korea's dependence on U.S. financial aid unsustainable at its current levels. As a result, the United States was not only interested in reducing its financial commitment to Korea but also in encouraging Japan to assume a more important aid role in providing the economic aid that South Korea needed.[32]

The United States's position was in complete contrast to Rhee's foreign policy orientation as the United States wanted his government not only to end its anti-Japan stance but more importantly move to establishing formal diplomatic relations with its former enemy. Naturally, this dissatisfaction the U.S. had with President Rhee was exacerbated because U.S. officials viewed him as ill-advisedly using economic American aid not just to prop up his regime but also to purchase consumption goods from the United States rather than investing in capital goods that could spur South Korea's economic development. At the same time, the United States wanted better South Korean-Japan relations because its plan was for Japan to replace the United States as Seoul's principal provider of economic aid. This was a foreign policy issue on which President Rhee was immovable and would, thus, remain a problem in U.S.-South Korean relations until the end of his administration in 1960.

The United States's frustrations with its South Korean ally continued to grow, and while there was talk among U.S. officials that American interests in South Korea would be better served by a change of administration, it would not be the United States that would end Rhee Syngman's tenure as South Korean President. Indeed, despite increasing levels of U.S. frustration with Rhee, it was his own domestic unpopularity that was his undoing. The growing unpopularity Rhee faced came to a head when the results of the 1960 election were announced.[33] The announcement that Rhee was the winner of a virtually unchallenged fourth term led to the widespread perception that the election was rigged, and protests broke out in numerous places after the results were announced. These protests threatened the Rhee government when students who were marching on the president's residence were fired on by police, killing as many as one hundred of the protesters. Immediately after this event, the United States, university professors in South Korea, and the Army's Chief of Staff called for the eighty-four-year old's resignation.

When the president resigned there was a rather short transition period that involved the installation of an interim president and then a newly elected president. This was an important time in terms of South Korea's domestic politics,[34] but it also heralded a change in the overall orientation of South Korea's foreign policy. One of the first announcements made by Foreign Minister, Chang Il-Huyng, is that there needed to be a readjustment in South Korea's approach to the region, especially with respect to the country's "attitude toward Japan and the nonaligned nations."[35] The foreign minister and other leaders advised that South Korea's security interests behooved better relations with Japan and other nations in the Asian region, and as a result Foreign Minister Chang recommended that South Korea improve its relations with Japan and the non-aligned nations of South and Southeast Asia. Change in the former president's foreign policy orientation had begun during this short democratic transition period, but it would take South Korea's next chief executive, General Park Chung-Hee, who came to power in a military coup, to bring these foreign policy changes to fruition, especially with respect to South Korea's relations with Japan.

General Park did not harbor the same level of animosity toward Japan as did his predecessor, and, as a result, he was agreeable to U.S requests for South Korea and Japan to mend relations and reestablish economic ties.[36] Fortunately, many of Japan's government leaders were also eager to get beyond their past differences and grow their country's economic ties with South Korea. Japan's elected leaders were also under pressure from business executives to reestablish economic interactions with South Korea in order to secure access to raw materials and to open markets for the export of finished Japanese goods. Japan's business leaders also wanted to have South Korea become a source of Japanese investment so that Japan could grow its own international trade. The problem, however, was that the San Francisco Treaty of 1952 ended formal hostilities between Japan and Korea, but it did not settle ongoing differences, which would require additional negotiations that would have to include an agreement on the amount of reparations Japan would need to provide.

As a result, the full reestablishment of economic and political relations between South Korea and Japan began with the Reparations Agreement of 1965, where Japan extended to the government of Park Chung-Hee $300 million in reparations, an additional $200 million in long-term credits, and a commitment for foreign direct investment from Japanese businesses that was close to the amount of reparations Japan would send to South Korea as part of this agreement. The result was a large initial sum of money extended to the South Korean government that elevated Japan to the status of the country's third largest donor. Although the amounts Japan extended to South Korea, did fluctuate widely over time, Japan remained a very important provider of economic aid to South Korea for some time. The growing importance of development assistance from Japan is captured in table 3.3. In one decade, Japan went from providing no aid to South Korea to almost 40 percent of the total amount of economic assistance that country received, and, by the end of the Cold War, economic assistance from Japan had increased to 80 percent of all the aid South Korea received.

Receiving aid from Japan was politically unpopular in South Korea, even under the authoritarian rule of Park Chung-Hee. Nonetheless, the former general felt that Japanese aid was necessary for his country's economic development goals. His government was interested in using the funds it received from Japan to expand South Korea's international trade, both with Japan and other countries. The Japanese government shared that goal and did not hide the view that principal purpose of its extending economic aid to South Korea was to serve Japan's economic interests by encouraging the development of trade between the two countries. A good part of the reparations money Japan extended to South Korea then had to be used for the purchase of goods and services produced in Japan.[37]

General Park's economic goals were not cryptic as well. He made it clear that his intention was to help the South Korean economy develop, and the focus of his strategy was to accomplish this by expanding South Korea's exports. The economic aid he received from Japan would help him accomplish this by providing resources to firms that would not only export back to Japan but develop as businesses so they to begin exporting to other nations as well. To accomplish this, however, it would be necessary for President Park to expand South Korea's diplomatic connections and make an effort to increase its international legitimacy as well.

The Correlates of War Diplomatic Exchange data reveal that President Park Chung-Hee established nearly twenty new diplomatic connections in the first five years of his presidency. These nations included politically friendly counties such as Australia, and the Netherlands, but they also include other nations that could begin to serve as recipients of South Korean exports. These nations were in the Middle East, Africa, and Central and South America, and what made them amenable to South Korean diplomacy and then trade was not just the economic benefits they would come to enjoy but also the fact that they were generally sympathetic with the U.S.-led camp in the international politics of the Cold War.

We see from table 3.1 that, before he was assassinated in 1979, President Park had established over fifty new embassies and twenty additional consuls that South Korea did not previously have. This is significant to be sure, but in the 1970s, several developments behooved President Park to reconsider his approach to nations which were previously off limits to formal diplomatic relations. Perhaps most important is the aftermath of South Korea's experience supporting the United States in the Vietnam War. The point is not just that South Korea supported American involvement but also that it actively participated in that conflict by sending as many as 50,000 soldiers to assist in U.S. operations on the ground. The fact that the United States's efforts in Vietnam ultimately failed is important in and of itself but what is more important is that South Korea's alignment with a failed U.S. strategy worked against Park's previous efforts to enhance his country's international legitimacy.

Evidence for this is witnessed in the fact that increasing international sympathy for the position of North Korea continued throughout the late-1960s. Giles (1996) presents votes on the pro-Seoul position for unification of the Korean Peninsula and the admission of the Democratic People's Republic of Korea (DPRK) to the United Nations from 1965 to 1975. His listing of votes on these two resolutions reveals how support for the North Korean position grew throughout this time, leading ultimately to the unification issue being removed from the agenda of the U.N. General Assembly and North Korea being admitted as a member of that body in 1973.[38] Giles (1996) also notes that the General Assembly at this time voted to disband the UNCURK, which the North claimed was biased in favor of the United States and Seoul. Moreover, he notes that the U.N. also passed a resolution to pursue a reunification of the peninsula that favored the North and called for the removal of U.S. troops in the South.

In addition to this, as U.S. involvement in Vietnam was winding down, then U.S. President, Richard Nixon, began his effort to seek rapprochement with the People's Republic of China. The warming of relations between the U.S. and China led to a shift in the dynamics of Cold War international relations. Specifically, the Sino-American rapprochement revealed the existence of a rift that had been growing between the Soviet Union and China. After an initial shock on the part of South Korea and the United States's other allies in Asia, there was a growing realization that the constraints originally in the Cold War Alliance system had loosened up, allowing South Korea and the other nations allied with the United States to expand their diplomatic connections. This loosening of international conditions and consideration of pursuing relations with nations that were previously off limits was facilitated by President Park's understanding that there was a limit to how many formal diplomatic relations he could establish if he continued in strict adherence to the Hallstein Doctrine.

These developments associated with the end of the Vietnam War and the United States's rapprochement with China represent the genesis of the second transition in South Korea's diplomatic relations. This is a transition in President Park's foreign policy thinking that relates to South Korea's diplomatic overtures to the communist world. The beginnings of this transition can be observed in earnest as early 1973 when Park announced "Korea's New Foreign Policy and Peace and Reunification." This announcement was an indication that South Korea would consider relaxing its adherence to the Hallstein Doctrine, and naturally, the two countries that would be most affected by this action would be the Soviet Union and the People's Republic of China.

This discussion of Seoul's relations with the communist world can be found in Ahn (1980) and Kihl (1991), who noted that the end of the Cold

War offered new opportunities for South Korea to establish diplomatic relations with nations with which it was previously unconnected. These countries included erstwhile communist nations that made the transition to democratic politics and market economics as well as those countries that continued to be communist, even those that continued to be diplomatically connected with North Korea. Naturally, such foreign policy efforts on the part of Seoul, particularly under the transitional president, Roh Tae-Woo, were encouraged further as the Cold War drew to a close. When he became president in 1988, Roh Tae-Woo established a northern focus (Nordpolotik) in his diplomatic efforts, which led his administration to numerous successes in establishing formal relationships with erstwhile allies of the Soviet Union such as Poland and Hungary. In contrast to such South Korean successes, the ending of the Cold War was much less kind to Pyongyang, which was increasingly forced to grapple with a loss of diplomatic and financial support from former benefactors, the Soviet Union in particular.[39]

The same is true for South Korea's efforts to improve relations with China, albeit Seoul's normalization of relations with Beijing proceeded more slowly than they did with Moscow. Efforts to establish relations with these two nations as well as other former communist nations of East Europe began with cultural and academic exchanges. Again, they were moved along by Roh Tae-Woo's Nordpolotik focus, which encouraged growth in trade that had begun to take off by throughout the 1980s. Ultimately, the initial efforts made by Park Chung-Hee paid off as his successors were able to establish formal diplomatic relations with the Soviet Union (1990) and China (1992). Indeed, building on Park's initial efforts, Roh Tae-Woo's Nordpolitik approach, taken together, put South Korea on a path to where it could continue to elevate itself into the influential middle power it is today.

Heo and Roehrig (2014) note that this dramatic change in South Korea's diplomatic relations with the communist world ". . . was possible thanks to South Korea's economic prosperity."[40] It is true that, when relations between South Korea and these two nations were established in the early 1990s, South Korea was experiencing rapid economic growth and was well on its way to being one of the world's most prosperous nations. Moreover, it is also true that leaders in the former Soviet Union and the People's Republic of China were motivated by South Korean investment and the economic benefits relations with the Asian Tiger would bring. Nonetheless, what this argument misses is that South Korea's leaders decided to approach the communist world well before it became the prosperous nation it is today. As a result, it was the efforts of President Park as leader of a still relatively poor country that paved the way for the increasing international influence South Korea enjoyed after the 1990s.

NOTES

1. The classic work on this is Waltz (1979).

2. The destructive potential of a superpower conflict was reinforced during the Cuban Missile Crisis which made clear the need for these two countries to be cautious with respect to any direct conflict. The classic work on the Cuban Missile Crisis by Graham Allison was reissued in 1999. See Allison and Zelikow (1999).

3. Again See Waltz (1979) and see also Mersheimer (1990).

4. The second instance of the Cold War turning hot in Asia is the Vietnam War, first a conflict where France attempted to reestablish its colonial regime in "Indo-china" and then with the involvement of the United States to prevent the establishment of a Communist government in the southern part of the country.

5. See e.g., Cummings (1997) and Seth (2011).

6. This does not mean they all followed the same course because, as we discuss in more detail in the following chapter, Korean presidents in the Cold War period followed different courses of action to achieve these goals.

7. This was Ban Ki-Moon who was the foreign minister under President Roh Mu-Hyun.

8. Again, see Ikenberry and Mo (2013).

9. This is not to deny the argument of such scholars as Heo and Roehrig (2014) who detail how South Korea's economic development affected its foreign policy but rather to emphasize what scholars who have championed this view have missed. Specifically, the path to South Korea's international influence was paved in the period of the Cold War before it became one of the world's largest economies.

10. The period of 1960 to 1961 is referred to as the Second Republic and Chang Myon is usually referred to as South Korea's chief executive at this time. He was clearly instrumental in establishing the Second Republic and the short period of democratic governance South Korea enjoyed at this time. However, Chang was prime minister and not president until forced from office in the coup that put Park Chung-Hee in office.

11. Park Chung-Hee established fifty-five formal diplomatic connections his nearly twenty-year administration.

12. This has become known as the Gwangju Massacre.

13. For clarification purposes, this section covers a period of time when the Korean Peninsula was not divided, which is why the subsection title refers to Korea and its diplomacy.

14. The Jurchens were an ethnically distinct people who occupied the region of Manchuria until the seventeenth century. Throughout this time, the Ryukyus refer to the islands of present day Okinawa and the Kingdom established there in the fifteenth century that was part of the Ming and Qing Dynasties tribute systems.

15. See e.g., Koo (1975).

16. See Gu (1995), p. 184.

17. See e.g., Seth (2011).

18. Japan entered a long period of self-imposed international isolation in 1603 when the Tokugawa Shogunate was established. This isolation formally ended in 1854 when the Americans forced Japan to sign the Treaty of Kanagawa.

19. We use the 2006 version of these data prepared by Bayer (2006) as our base. Overall, these data include formal exchanges between pairs of nations at the ambassador, minister, and charge d'affaires levels. They include all dyadic exchanges in five year intervals between 1844 to 1914, 1920 to 1940, and 1950 to 2002. Prior to 1844, these data record dyadic exchanges for the years 1817, 1824, 1827, 1832, 1836, and 1840. See also, Singer and Small (1966 and 1973) and Bayer (2007).

20. For a discussion of how diplomatic exchange scores were calibrated for this period, see Singer and Small (1966).

21. The Korean Peninsula north of the 38th parallel had been occupied by the Soviet Union prior to the formal surrender of Japan.

22. South Korea established formal relations with the United Kingdom in January 1949 and France one month later. A short time later in March, Korea and the Philippines established embassies in each other's capitals.

23. By formal diplomatic connections, we are referring to countries in which South Korea had established embassies. The nations with which it had relations were by and large U.S. allies in the Cold War.

24. This concept is discussed in more detail below.

25. In addition to the number of embassies South Korea opened, the Correlates of War Diplomatic Exchange Data also include the number of Counsels, and Charge d'Affairs that South Korea sent abroad as well as the number of resident representatives it sent to such international organizations as ASEAN and OECD.

26. For the post-armistice period, this was the United States.

27. This drop corresponds to the end of the Vietnam War, specifically, the loss of previously established diplomatic partners that the communist reunion of North and South Vietnam caused and the reaction of certain nations to South Korea's military involvement there.

28. This is generally true except for Japan with which South Korea did not establish diplomatic relations until 1965.

29. Syngman Rhee earned a B.A. degree from George Washington University, an MA degree from Harvard University, and a PhD from Princeton University.

30. See Newnham (2002) on South Korea using U.S. diplomatic facilities.

31. See e.g., Kuznets (1975) and Steinberg (1985).

32. At the same time, most of Japan's leaders were interested in stabilizing the regional environment for security and realized that this would require solving outstanding problems with Korea.

33. First, Rhee changed the South Korean constitution so he could stand for a fourth term. Moreover, results indicated that he obtained nearly 100 percent of the vote because his opponent, Cho Pyong-Ok died several weeks before the election was held, and this occurred amidst reports that the election's results were rigged. Nohlen et. al., (2001).

34. Many observers have noted that the removal of Rhee Syngman meant that South Korea was making the transition to democracy. However, due to the instability

of the presidency Yun Bo-Seon and Prime Minister Chang Myon, this democratic period was very short lived. See e.g., Kim (1975) and Seth (2010).

35. See Kim (1975: 216).

36. This was to include Japan replacing the United States as Korea's principal source of economic aid.

37. This was also true for subsequent economic aid that was delivered in the form of grants.

38. Giles (1996) also notes that the General Assembly at this time voted to disband the UNCURK, which the North claimed was biased in favor of the United States and Seoul. Moreover, he notes that the U.N. also passed a resolution to pursue a reunification of the peninsula that favored the North and called for the removal of U.S. troops in the South.

39. We should note here that Korea's post-Cold War diplomatic successes were the beneficiary of efforts made during the Cold War when Korea abandoned adherence to the Hallstein Doctrine and allowed such contacts as those involving academics, culture, and trade. Contacts at this time eased the way for deeper economic and trade contacts which then helped Seoul move to a point where formal diplomatic relations could be realized. Again, see Kim (1997).

40. Heo and Roehrig (2014:67)

Chapter Four

Post-Cold War Diplomacy and the Path to International Influence

In 1989 and 1990, a series of events unfolded that presaged the occurrence of a sea change in international relations. Perhaps most important was the demolition of the Berlin Wall that had separated that German city into East and West Zones since 1961. The demolition took place in November, 1989, and, less than a month later, Soviet Premiere Mikhail Gorbachev and U.S. President George H.W. Bush met in Malta where Gorbachev declared that he would not initiate a "hot" war with the United States to maintain the loyalty of the Soviet Union's vassal states in Eastern Europe. This historic announcement was quickly followed by the holding of multi-party elections in many of this region's countries, where Soviet military might had long kept them in Moscow's sphere of influence. In July of 1990, the Communist Party of the Soviet Union announced that it would end its monopoly of power in that country, and these watershed events were then followed by the reunification of Germany in October.

These developments signaled the end of the Cold War, and they had an immediate and profound impact on the regional politics of Europe and the West in general. Indeed, the end of the Cold War in many ways created hope that a more peaceful and prosperous world where political competition—both domestic and international—would be more free and the threat of nuclear war would be reduced if not significantly diminished. In the immediate aftermath of the Cold War, the United States stood as the planet's only superpower, a consequence of the Soviet Union's collapse, and this fact engendered this hope and led nations to begin emphasizing economic issues as the principal focus of their respective domestic and international policy efforts. Moreover, as some observers have opined, the demolition of the Berlin Wall, which had long served as a political-economic and ideological divide as much as it functioned as a physical barrier sectioning off two different worlds in the same

European city, symbolized the triumph of democratic principles and practices and market economics in most of the world's nations.[1]

To be sure, the end of the Cold War was also important in East Asia, but its impact was less direct to be sure. We can best understand its implications as an event that would offer both opportunities and challenges for the nations of the East Asian region, but we must also note that the end of the Cold War's impact on East Asia was not as profound as it was in Europe. This is because interstate relations in East Asia had long rested on certain continuities that would remain in place up to the present day. Clearly, there were political openings that led to more democratic political practices, particularly in South Korea and Taiwan, and there were new opportunities for expanded economic interactions, especially with China and the former Soviet Union.

These changes augured a more peaceful and prosperous region, but, again, their impact was enervated by certain conditions that did not change with the end of the Cold War in Europe. Most notable of these continuities is the fact that the East Asian region is unique in being the one part of the world where Cold War conflicts have persisted. Specifically, the Korean peninsula has remained divided with competing regimes in Seoul and Pyongyang; there is an ongoing sovereignty conflict between China and Taiwan; and the dispute over the rightful possessor of the four islands north of Hokkaido between Japan and Russia continues even in a post-Soviet era.[2]

The concurrence of both challenges and opportunities in the wake of the Cold War's end is the situation in which the South Korean leadership found itself in 1989 and beyond. The new opportunities that leaders in Seoul enjoyed involved South Korea being less constrained internationally by Cold War alliances and possessing more economic and political wherewithal to achieve its international goals. The challenges South Korean leaders faced were both domestic and international, where the former involved leaders being forced to grapple with structural adjustments in its rapidly growing economy while, at the same time, being be more concerned with domestic political pressures because of its transition to democracy in the late 1980s. This represented a very different policy environment compared to that faced by earlier South Korean leaders, like Park Chung-Hee, who could design and implement policies with fewer domestic constraints. Internationally, these challenges involved determining how to put South Korea's emerging middle power status to best use in service of the interests of the Korean people and, perhaps more importantly, how to meet this challenge while navigating the power transition that was occurring in Northeast Asia with a rising China, a persistently challenging relationship with Japan, and evolving relationships with Washington and Pyongyang, aspects of which were unpredictable and sometimes unsettling.

To understand clearly the impact that the end of the Cold War had on South Korea's rise to international influence, we will first need to map its evolving relationships, both with the nations of the world as well as international organizations with which South Korea would join and increasingly influence. In this effort, we will address how South Korea's leaders responded to the new opportunities and challenges that the end of the Cold War presented while, at the same time, continuing to be focused on ongoing issues, like inter-Korean relations, that remained prevalent from 1989 to the present day. In this effort, we will also focus on how the leadership of South Korea continued to elevate the international influence of South Korea by building on the domestic and international achievements the country's leadership mounted earlier in the post-armistice period and continuing to elevate itself into the prosperous and internationally influential nation it is today. This will naturally include discussion of specific post-Cold War developments in the country's diplomatic and trading relations and the roles these played in its international rise.

SOUTH KOREA IN A POST-COLD WAR WORLD

In his 2010 annual radio address, South Korean President Lee Myung-Bak stated that his nation "successfully transformed itself from a passive follower into an active agenda-setter."[3] He was referring to how South Korea had not only become a full-fledged member of numerous international organizations but also a member with a growing influence on the policy directives guiding these international organizations. South Korea's memberships included such important regional international organizations as the Asian Development Bank, the ASEAN Regional Forum, and the Asian Pacific Economic Cooperation forum but also a number of United Nations sponsored institutions like UN Peacekeeping operations, the Food and Agricultural Organization, and the International Labor Organization. By 2010, it also became one of the most important middle powers to achieve membership on the Development Assistance Committee (DAC) of the Organization for Economic Cooperation and Development, the most important international organization for the distribution of economic aid in the world.

It was during the post-Cold War era that South Korea left no doubt that it had become a prosperous member of the family of advanced industrial democracies, influencing the policies of many of the world's most important international organizations. It accomplished this because it had become a truly prosperous nation, one that not only produced and exported capital and high quality finished goods, but also a nation whose transition from poverty to prosperity came to be a model of successful economic development that could be emulated by the world's less developed economies.

It also accomplished this because South Korea continued to expand the number of countries with which it would establish and maintain formal diplomatic relations, and these included many countries that were erstwhile adversaries. This growing number of diplomatic relations naturally helped South Korean business leaders rapidly and significantly increase the volume of international trade in which they engaged, and this in turn accelerated the growth of South Korea's domestic economy, increasing the prosperity of the South Korean people. These ongoing developments, taken together, allowed South Korea to show the world that its influence in international affairs was positive and real and that it would become more involved in the policy making process of those international organizations in which it had memberships.

In the years after the fall of the Berlin Wall, South Korea faced new challenges and opportunities, and its leaders faced this by continuing to build on the domestic and international accomplishments its leaders achieved in the early part of the post-armistice period. This does not mean that all post-Cold War leaders approached the new challenges and opportunities they faced in the same way because some post-Cold War presidents pursued somewhat different foreign and domestic policy priorities, especially with respect to North Korea. Nonetheless, all of South Korea's leaders at this time endeavored to meet the new challenges they encountered while taking advantage of the opportunities that the end of the Cold War in Europe presented them to continue building South Korea's international connections and expanding its economic interactions around the globe. Consequently, regardless of how they approached North Korea, South Korean leaders in the post-Cold War era all helped to accelerate their country's international rise.

It is important to note here that, while continuing to expand their nation's formal diplomatic connections and trading relations in the years after the end of the Cold War, South Korean leaders added an additional emphasis to their efforts to elevate South Korea internationally. It is the case that, in the wake of the events of 1989, South Korean leaders focused on becoming more active and influential in many important international organizations. As mentioned briefly above, while some of these activities did include work to enhance the international security environment through greater levels of participation in such things as U.N. peacekeeping operations and international efforts to curb nuclear proliferation, South Korea's most notable achievements rested on its growing involvement in international organizations dedicated to the economic affairs of the world.

This is particularly true for South Korea's efforts to help the world's largest economies coordinate their economic aid policies, influencing the manner in which the world's advanced industrial democracies distribute their economic wealth and political influence for the benefit of the world's less fortunate nations. This new emphasis on international organizations naturally required great diplomatic skill, like that displayed by its leaders in the wake of the Korean War. However, in addition to this, this new emphasis also required that South Korea employ growing amounts of wealth that its rapidly growing economy would produce. This is particularly true for South Korea becoming an increasingly influential member of such important international organizations as the Development Assistance Committee (DAC) of the OECD, and, the G20.

In light of this, our specific purpose in this chapter is to show how, from 1989 to the present, South Korea's leaders accelerated their country's international rise by focusing on their country's growing involvement in select international organizations, which South Korean leaders achieved by taking advantage of the new domestic and international opportunities they enjoyed with the end of the Cold War, but, at the same time, by overcoming the challenges that both their changed domestic political dynamics as well as altered system of international relations presented them in the post-cold War period. We will be specific in our discussion of the new opportunities and constraints with which South Korea's leaders had to contend and divide them into the domestic and international levels on which they existed. By mapping these new factors that molded the efforts of this country's leaders to continue growing its domestic prosperity and elevating its international status, we can more clearly demonstrate how South Korea continued on the path it paved in the early post-armistice period but also were able to shift the country's international efforts to influencing the operation of many important international organizations.

This effort begins with a discussion of the new challenges and opportunities South Korean leaders faced throughout the post-Cold War years. These opportunities and challenges were both domestic and international, each of which involved new dynamics that were both political and economic. We start this discussion by focusing on changes that the post-Cold War period brought at the domestic level.

DOMESTIC CHALLENGES AND OPPORTUNITIES

Perhaps the most notable domestic development that affected South Korea in the post-Cold War era involved its transformation from a strongly authoritarian state to a fully consolidated democratic political system. South Korea's political transformation, while often taking a back seat to its economic ascendance in the scholarly literature, was a truly remarkable event. Because it remained in a virtual state of war after the 1953 armistice, domestic forces that were opposed to the country's democratization enjoyed a position of political strength, rendering the emergence of democratic politics not just difficult but unlikely, even in the long term. Moreover, as South Korea became more and more prosperous, the South Korean state also got stronger, generating more wherewithal to serve its own interests. Finally, until the transition began in earnest in 1987, South Korea was governed by a political elite that was at time wont to engage in repression when it found its fundamental interests as rulers of the nation threatened.

This authoritarian advantage, which persisted long after the Armistice of 1953, does not mean that there were no attempts by opposition movements to make the country more democratic but rather that the status quo was maintained in large part by the strength of the authoritarian leadership. To be sure, there were elections to the Korean presidency and to the country's National Assembly, and there were also civil movements that advocated for greater levels of democracy. However, the authoritarian government of South Korea during this period achieved its power through coups and maintained it with the aid of a very strong and alert military. As a result, movements advocating democratization were suppressed, and sometimes brutally.[4]

This pattern of successful repression to any regime challenge in South Korea persisted until the late 1980s. It was at this time that, once again, South Korea witnessed movements that advocated for greater levels of democracy. The pro-democracy movement of the late 1980s, however, was different from those that occurred earlier, even the one that had occurred in Kwangju in 1980. The most recent movement for democracy was not a limited, regional affair, and it ultimately came to include broad swaths of South Korean society. As a result it was less easily repressed and resulted in a complete transition to democratic politics in a South Korea where strongly authoritarian traditions gave little hope for such a transition.

The changes that occurred in South Korean political institutions and processes are clearly reflected in measures political scientists use to capture a country's level of democracy.[5] As shown in figure 4.1, until the early 1980s, South Korea received some of the lowest possible scores on the Polity IV and Freedom House scales. From this time to 1987, South Korea's level of democracy was upgraded slightly but still remained solidly undemocratic. These negative Polity IV and Freedom House scores changed at the end of the decade when the country successfully transitioned to democracy, after which it continued to solidify its democracy, earning very high, positive scores on both indicators. The point is that, unlike other countries struggling with the democratization process, once the transition occurred in South Korea, there was no turning back as its new democratic politics became stronger and more consolidated as time elapsed.

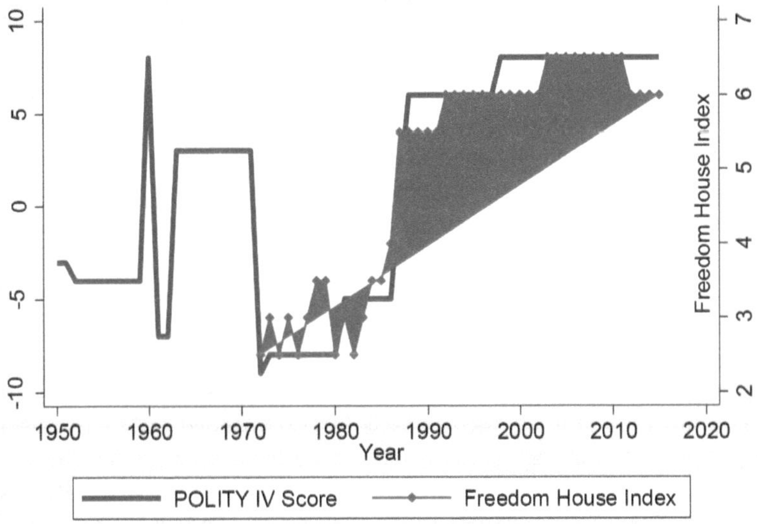

Figure 4.1. Changes in the Level of Democracy in South Korea, 1950–2015.

What is interesting about South Korea's political transformation is not just that it resulted in a consolidated democracy as quickly as it did, but rather why the democratization movement in the late 1980s was successful but earlier attempts were not. As stated briefly above, South Korea experienced numerous movements for political change prior to the late-1980s. Indeed, the Japanese surrender to the United States south of the 38th parallel at the end of the Pacific War was immediately followed by citizen movements to establish a new, democratic regime in an independent Korea.[6] These movements involved extensive citizen participation that often met with repressive efforts that sometimes became violent. As stated above, South Korea's movement for democracy of the late 1980s, however, led to an entirely different outcome despite the fact that it challenged an increasingly strong authoritarian state that initially responded with repression and some violence. This raises the interesting question of why the late 1980s produced such a different political outcome.

Our answer to this is how South Korea's twin successes of growing its formal diplomatic connections and expanding its international trade are essential components. Moreover, it was how these twin successes led to growing domestic prosperity in South Korea that made successful democratization virtually inevitable. The theory behind how such developments come together to produce successful democratic transitions begins with the seminal work of Stolper and Samuelson (1947) on the impact that trade protection had on real wages in order to explain who gains and who loses from expansions of free trade. This is the well-known Stolper-Samuelson Theorem which, in conjunction with the Heckscher-Ohlin general equilibrium framework out of which it was derived, posited that owners and intensive users of abundant factors will gain from expansions of free trade while owners and intensive users of scarce factors will benefit from protection. This means that, when the growing establishment of formal diplomatic relations leads to the expansion of a recipient country's international trade,[7] the owners and intensive users of that country's abundant factors will benefit economically while the owners and intensive users of that country's scarce factors will be hurt economically.

What is important about this for the case of South Korea's political transformation is the parallel idea that expansions and contractions of international trade can be partner to profound political implications. As Rogowski (1989) noted in his seminal work, the beneficiaries of expanded trade will endeavor to maintain and promote its expansion,[8] while those who are hurt by expansions of trade will prefer to stop it and seek protection.[9] Moreover, Rogowski (1989) noted that, as the beneficiaries of expanded trade become more economically powerful, they also become better able to engage in the political action necessary to advocate for maintaining the expanded trade that provided them with increased economic benefits in the first place. This means that such groups become more able to overcome the collective action obstacles they encounter in attempts to maintain their increased wealth and growing power, but it also means that they increasingly acquire the wherewithal to defend and promote their own political interests.

These observations lead to a set of expectations about how international trade that expands because a nation increases its formal relations around the world will affect the political dynamics of that nation. To illustrate this more fully, we must first define the groups that are in power versus those that are potential challengers. While undoubtedly oversimplified, we begin with a simple definition of power relations in an authoritarian country, like pre-democratic South Korea, by dividing economically (factor) based groups into those that are within the authoritarian government's distributional coalition and those that are potential challengers to that government. We next assume that the total amount of political power (PT) in the authoritarian country being examined can be represented as the sum of the power possessed by the government and its distributional coalitions, P_G, and those who would be challengers, P_{CH}. This distinction leads to the following identity, $PT = P_G + P_{CH}$.[10]

Before a growing number of diplomatic relations helps increase a nation's international trade, we assume that the owners and intensive users of those factors who support the government will be more powerful than the owners and intensive users of factors who do not. Expressing this relationship as a ratio, we have $P_G / P_{CH} > 1$. Given that successful diplomatic efforts result in increased international trade, power relations between government supporters and challengers may change, and this depends on whether government groups and potential challengers are the owners/intensive users of abundant or scarce factors. When the owners and intensive users of the recipient country's abundant factors are within the authoritarian government's distributional coalition, increased trade will benefit the authoritarian government economically, increasing its ability to maintain itself in that country's dominant political position. Under such circumstances, diplomacy that leads to expanded international trade is very unlikely to lead to democratization. Specifically, this is the scenario where increased diplomacy and trade is least likely to lead to a democratic transition as it represents the case where the post-trade growth power ratio is greater than the pre-trade growth power ratio, that is, $(P_G / P_{CH})_t < (P_G / P_{CH})_{t+n}$.[11]

On the other hand, when the owners and intensive users of the recipient country's abundant factors are potential challengers to an incumbent authoritarian government, receiving foreign aid that increases trade will help create the conditions that make a democratic transition more likely. This is because, as diplomatic successes help increase the level of international trade in which a recipient country engages, the result will be not only an increase in the wealth of the potential challengers but also a growth in their overall political wherewithal. These changes will result in shifts in the relative power of these two sets of groups, which will then raise the likelihood that the benefitted groups will challenge the government and perhaps initiate a democratic transition. This is the scenario where diplomacy and increased trade is likely to lead to a democratic transition, that is, when the post-trade growth power ratio is less than the pre-trade growth power ratio or $(P_G / P_{CH})_t > (P_G / P_{CH})_{t+n}$.

With these relationships defined, we now have a set of expectations about how the diplomatic successes of South Korea's leaders during the Cold War period helped ultimately pave the way for the country's transition to democracy. In the case of post-armistice South Korea, increased diplomacy and trade rendered a democratic transition more likely because potential challengers to that country's authoritarian government were the owners or intensive users of the country's abundant factors, and they were not part of that government's distributional coalitions. During the early post-armistice period, South Korea possessed a growing supply of increasingly skilled and educated labor. In fact, labor was South Korea's abundant factor, and, when studies of the country's economy analyze its post-armistice patterns of growth, they focus on its labor market and note that South Korea is a late developer that never experienced a scarcity of labor.[12] This was true during the colonial period, and it remains true throughout the Cold War years. Perhaps the best evidence for this is the fact that the Korean economy was not able to absorb all available labor early on in the post-armistice period. One study of the Korean economy noted that, in 1960, as much as 20 percent of Korea's industrial and agricultural labor force was unemployed.[13]

What complicated this problem of labor underemployment, especially early on in the post-armistice period, is the fact that the South Korean workforce continued to grow which helped to maintain a surplus in the country's labor supply. However, as the South Korean economy expanded and international trade assumed higher proportions of the country's GDP, excess labor became increasingly absorbed. This growing absorption of labor helped push wages up, even though they were strictly controlled by the government, and this in turn led to benefits accruing to South Korean labor witnessed in a number of measures of worker and middle-class wellbeing. In light of the theoretical perspective set out above, we would expect South Korean labor as the country's abundant factor to experience increasing economic and political benefits as the country's level of international trade increased.

Consider the data in figure 4.2, which reveal the dramatic growth that occurred in the country's real GDP per worker. Specifically, between 1972 and 1995, this growth was over 250 percent from well under $7,500 to over $25,000. This increasing prosperity of South Korean workers led to more demands for the ability of workers to organize for their specific interests and to

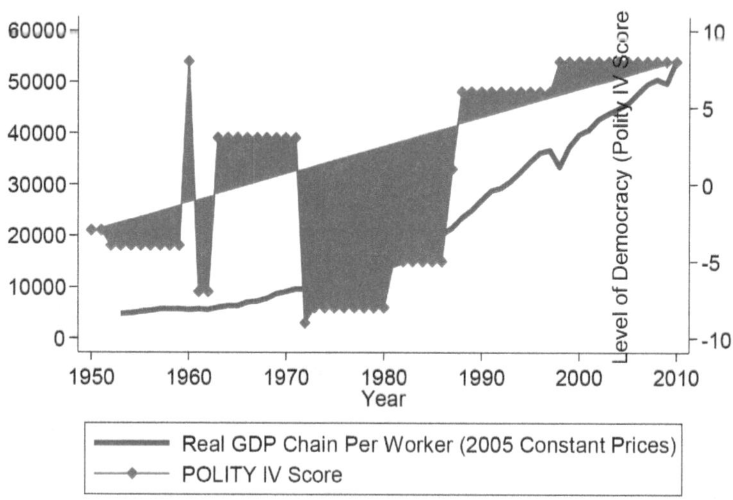

Figure 4.2. Expanded Wealth of the Korean Working Class and the Expansion of Political Rights, 1950–2010.

take action to promote these interests.[14] Over the long term, this pressure was aided by the fact that laborers became more prosperous and, thus, possessive of the wherewithal to be more politically active and able to advocate more effectively for their essential interests. This resulted in South Korean workers obtaining increased political rights, as indicated by the corresponding rise in democracy in figure 4.1. Specifically, South Korean workers were able to secure a limited expansion of political rights in the 1980s, corresponding to the wealth gains they experienced from the country's growing international trade. However, the expansion of political rights they experienced was at its greatest when the country transitioned to and consolidated its democracy. Again, this process would not have been possible without labor, as the country's abundant factor, experiencing the economic gains it did from the country's rapidly growing international trade.

While South Korea's turn to democracy was undoubtedly a good thing for the citizens of this county, it did result in somewhat changed political dynamics that made the conduct of foreign policy somewhat more complicated in the post-Cold War era than earlier when strong presidents were in power. Unlike foreign policy decision making under strong presidents, like Park Chung-Hee, presidents after the transition to democracy had to speak to an electorate on which they relied for support. This meant that other issues like the distribution of economic wealth, corruption, and expansions of the welfare state would play a more prominent role in the policy making process. This naturally led to some disagreements between political parties and groups of the left versus the right, but the greatest differences dividing South Korean politics with respect to foreign policy had to do with how best to approach the regime in Pyongyang.

In addition to South Korea's remarkable political transformation, the patterns of economic growth that we witnessed in the years of the Cold War continued throughout the post-Cold War period. In fact, economic growth accelerated as did the expansion of South Korean trade. Data on Korea's economic growth is shown in figure 4.3, and they reveal very clearly that the growth of the South Korean economy, which picked up in the later years of the Cold War period, accelerated over the next several decades. Patterns of South Korean economic growth can perhaps be best described as an increasing expansion of its per capita GDP with each succeeding decade.[15]

Specifically, as mentioned in the previous chapter, in the decade of the 1960s, South Korea was undoubtedly a poor country as its per capita GDP was less than $200. In the following decade, Korea remained a relatively poor country even though its per capita GDP more than doubled to just less than $500. By the 1980s, however, Korea had begun to become more prosperous as growth in its per capita GDP accelerated to over $5,000. Although it suf-

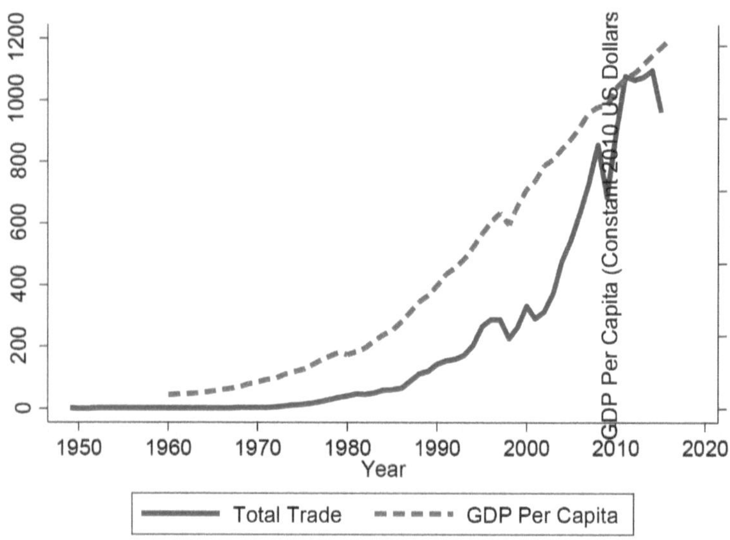

Figure 4.3. Trade and Per Capita GDP in South Korea, 1950–2015.

fered economic declines in the next two decades due to the Won Crisis of the mid 1990s and the financial crisis of 2008,[16] Korea's per capita GDP has continued to increase. Its per capita GDP is now over $27,000 and in the last couple of years has slowed in the amount it expands each year.

NEW INTERNATIONAL CHALLENGES AND OPPORTUNITIES

As we also noted in the previous chapter, the expansion of South Korean trade followed a similar pattern. Although growth in South Korea's trade took off earlier than did the country's GDP growth because of the economic assistance it received early in the post-Armistice period, it nonetheless expanded in much the same way as did per capita GDP growth. Specifically, we see from the data in figure 4.3 throughout the post-Cold War years, South Korean trade experienced two periods of expanded growth. In 1960, Korea's total international trade was just over $300 million, but, ten years later, it had grown by over 900 percent to over $2.8 billion. In the next decade, South Korea's total trade grew even faster—over 1000 percent—to $40 billion, and, in the next two decades, South Korea's total international trade continued to grow but at somewhat lower rates. In the 1980s, total trade grew by over 300 percent, and, between 1990 and 2000, growth dropped to just over 200 percent.

We see from the data in figure 4.4 that, as growth in South Korea's GDP accelerated in the post-Cold War years, so did growth in its Gross National Income (GNI).[17] Indeed, we see that the relationship between the expansion of international trade and the rise in South Korea's GNI is equally strong as it is with GDP.[18] Gross National Income is an excellent indicator of South Korea's overall prosperity, and, like the case of per capita GDP, this remains true at one and five year time lags as well as others.[19]

What this extensive growth in South Korea's GDP and GNI indicates is that post-Cold War leaders in South Korea had more economic resources to deploy in service of the country's international political and economic goals. These additional economic resources would be essential if South Korea were to accelerate its international rise to influence for two reasons. First, this is true because it would need to bring more benefits to the new countries with which it would enter diplomatic relations and parallel with this is the fact that the types of countries with which it would begin trading would require more direct investment. This is because they tended to be either former communist countries or among the world's least developed economies. Second, as South Korean leaders shifted their focus to becoming more involved in selected international organizations, they would have to employ more economic resources to this end.[20]

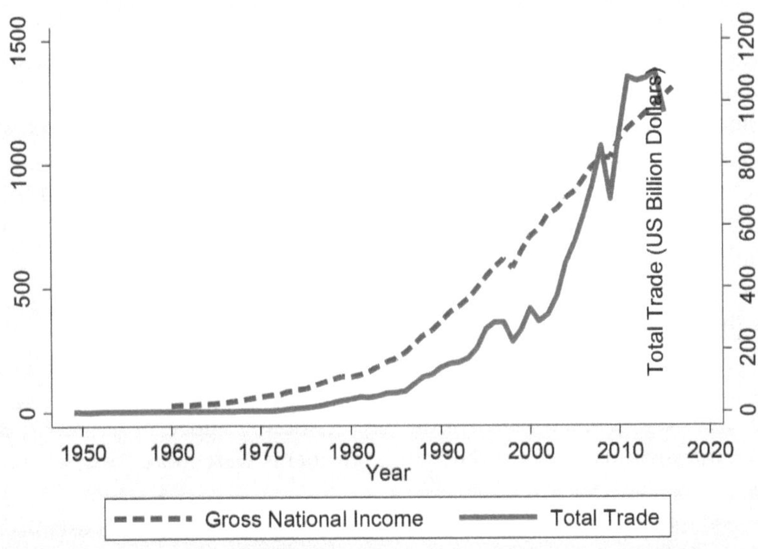

Figure 4.4. Trade and Gross National Income, 1950–2015.

The end of the Cold War in Europe signaled an era of unprecedented opportunity for South Korean leaders to continue to elevate their nation internationally. The most important reason for this is that the strict and hierarchical alliance system that governed international relations throughout the years of the Cold War had not only loosened up but had virtually ended with the collapse of the Soviet Union. This gave leaders of South Korea the opportunity to establish formal relations with nations that were previously off limits and, thus, to continue to expand trading relations, increasing the number of countries with which South Korea would have economic interactions.

To be sure, South Korea entered this period of new international opportunities poised to accelerate its international rise, but it also began the post-Cold War effort leaving no doubt as to just how much it was already on the way elevated its international status. One year after South Korea made the transition to democratic politics, it became the host of the 1988 Summer Olympics, a decision that not only revealed how far South Korea had come politically and economically but also how it was surpassing its adversary in the North in terms of its international reputation. Further evidence for South Korea's progress is witnessed in the fact that the United Nations recognized a two-Korea policy and allowed both Seoul and Pyongyang to have seats in the General Assembly, something Pyongyang was vehemently against. This does not mean that Seoul ignored its adversary in the North because at this time it initiated a new dialogue with the regime north of the 38th parallel. The specific reference here is to Roh Tae-Woo's Nord Politics where, in addition to focusing on a more productive dialogue with Pyongyang, he also looked to South Korea establishing more relations with communist and formerly communist countries.

The specific diplomatic accomplishments of South Korea's post-Cold War presidents are contained in table 4.1.[21] Even though a significant percentage of South Korea's current level of diplomatic relations had been established before the demolition of the Berlin Wall, post-Cold War presidents continued expanding South Korea's formal diplomatic ties. Although Roh Tae-Woo was president from 1988 to 1993 and, thus, was in office both during and after the Cold War, we begin with Kim Young-Sam, who succeeded Roh in 1993. As we see from the data, South Korea continued to establish formal diplomatic relations with new countries all throughout the years following the Cold War. While each president during this period added to South Korea's formal international connections, some presidents were more successful than others.

Indeed, nearly two-thirds of the formal diplomatic connections established after the Cold War ended were effected by South Korea's two progressive or left-leaning presidents. These were Kim Dae-Jung and Roh Moo-Hyun, who

Table 4.1. Diplomatic Successes of South Korea's Presidents in the Post-Cold War Period

Presidents	*Embassies*	*Consuls*	*Representatives*	*Total*
Kim Young-Sam	4	2	1	7
Kim Dae-Jung	6	8	1	15
Roh Moo-Hyun	9	9	0	18
Lee Myung-Bak	41	4	1	9
Park Geun-hye	10	1	0	2

Source: Compiled by the authors from the Diplomatic Missions Established by Year.

created and implemented what is known as South Korea's Sunshine Policy. While known in the popular discourse as the Sunshine Policy, its official name was the Reconciliation and Cooperation Policy. It was designed and implement first by President Kim Dae-Jung, who was awarded the Nobel Peace Prize for his efforts, and continued by his successor, Roh Moo-Hyun. The genesis of the policy was to increase communications between Pyongyang and Seoul, which the policy was successful at implementing. Indeed, throughout these two presidential administrations, there was increased dialogue and even two North-South summits, one in June 2000 and the other in October of 2007. Another part of this policy's genesis is witnessed in the growing economic gap between North and South. To help bridge this gap, this policy involved a number of cooperative business ventures.

While these two presidents succeeded in establishing most of the formal diplomatic ties that South Korea would effect during this period, the presidents just before (Kim Young-Sam) and just after (Lee Myung-Bak) together connected with just under a third of those established at this time. These points tell us is that there are differences in the quantities of diplomatic successes these post-Cold War presidents had, but there was one feature to the diplomatic efforts of presidents at this time that characterized all post-Cold War presidents. Specifically, what characterized all of the diplomatic efforts made during these years is the type of nation with which South Korea would seek to establish and maintain formal diplomatic relations. Most notable during this period was those nations that were formerly communist powers, be they part of the former Soviet Union or communist nations in other parts of the world like East, Southeast, or Central Asia. There were also a number of less developed nations that were added to South Korea's diplomatic connections at this time, particularly in Africa.

Being well on its way to becoming a prosperous and influential middle power during this period, South Korea could employ more economic resources in service of its diplomatic efforts and, thus, actions to increase the scope of international business its companies could conduct. In addition to this, it was in this post-Cold War period that South Korea increased its presence in a number of international institutions and processes, and this success would not have been possible without it being well on its way to becoming the prosperous nations it is today. These involved numerous international organizations and, as mentioned briefly above, they involved both regional institutions as well as international organizations that were truly global. We focus on one of these successes, the one that best symbolizes how South Korea's increasing wealth was employed to accelerate its influence in the world's most important policy making bodies. Specifically, we focus on South Korea's membership in the Development Assistance Committee (DAC) of the OECD.

The phrase, Official Development Assistance (ODA), traces its origins to the late 1960s when members of the Development Assistance Committee (DAC) of the Organization for Economic Cooperation and Development (OECD) agreed that economic aid should adhere to specific criteria.[22] Specifically, economic aid must be provided by an officially sanctioned government agency that distributes the aid principally for the purpose of economic development in the recipient nation. Moreover, economic aid must be structured in a concessional manner, which means it is offered at terms that are more generous to recipient nations than would be possible if distributed strictly by the market.[23] Despite the fact that all ODA must adhere to these criteria so that it assists recipient nations in their development efforts, nations also employ ODA to promote their own domestic economic and international interests.[24]

What is unique about South Korea's becoming an influential donor nation is not simply that it is a relatively new member of the group of developed nations,[25] which rapidly rose to this status in the post-armistice period, but rather that it is the only member of the OECD's prestigious Development Assistance Committee (DAC) to ascend to this group of donor nations after being a recipient of economic assistance for several decades.[26] South Korea's earliest ODA contributions were disbursed in obeisance to its own economic development needs.[27] It has been referred to as one of the East Asian Developmental States, which, like Japan, rendered domestic economic development goals supreme among all other policy priorities.[28] Developing its own economy remained the paramount goal, but South Korea's leaders also faced certain international challenges. Most important was the fact that the armistice left it in the situation of being isolated internationally. As we have discussed above, in the early post-armistice period, South Korea was forced to share some of its diplomatic facilities with the United States,[29] and, while trying to develop its own economy, South Korean leaders worked to reconnect their nation to the international community.[30]

Although achieving DAC membership only recently (2010), South Korea is like other DAC-member nations in that its ODA programs are administered by more than one government agency.[31] The first of these is the Ministry of Foreign Affairs and Trade (MOFAT), which oversees South Korea's ODA programs to ensure that they are conducted in accordance with all applicable laws as well as Seoul's diplomatic and security policies. This means that MOFAT officials are more interested in using South Korea ODA for diplomatic purposes such as promoting the international goals of the country than purely domestic interests.[32] In 1991, the MOFAT created the Korea International Cooperation Agency (KOICA) to manage all of South Korea's ODA that is distributed in the form of grants and to help ensure that grant aid and technical assistance programs effectively promote sustainable development in recipient nations. In 2011, MOFAT and KOICA were jointly responsible for 37 percent of South Korea's total Official Development Assistance disbursements.

The second agency responsible for the disbursement of ODA in the form of loans is the Ministry of Strategy and Finance (MOSF). This agency seeks to ensure that South Korea's ODA is effective at promoting international economic cooperation,[33] and it accomplishes its supervision of ODA loans through South Korea's Export-Import Bank, which oversees the nation's Economic Development Cooperation Fund (EDCF). What this means is that this agency's officials are most interested in using the nation's ODA to promote South Korea's economic development interests.[34] In 2011, 42 percent of Korea's total ODA was provided in the form of loans.

Finally, there are other government agencies that participated in the distribution of economic assistance, but this aid has remained around one-fifth of Korea's total disbursements. Most important would be the South Korean Presidency or the Blue House.[35] The Blue House has influenced South Korea's distribution of ODA in three particular ways. Two are relatively minor and involve, first, adjudicating disputes between competing ODA agencies in terms of the amounts they can distribute, and the second concerns the discretionary money the Blue House uses for specific international projects. Where the Blue House has the most influence is in the overall approach South Korea will take in allocating economic assistance to its northern adversary, North Korea. We see that the presidencies of Kim Dae-Jung and Roh Mu-Hyun pursued the "Sunshine Policy," which involved a more open approach to Pyongyang both diplomatically and in terms of offering aid for to enhance this more open diplomacy.

These two sets of government agencies involved competing discourses with respect to the actual distribution of ODA disbursements, The first is what Kim (2016) called the "Intellectual Leadership" approach, which argued that, given South Korea's unique experience of moving from a recipient to a developed, donor nation, it should develop and implement ODA policies that are informed by this very important experience. This discourse has been developed and promoted by the Ministry of Strategy and Finance (MOSF), and has been supported by South Korea's corporate world, think tanks, and its Export-Import Bank. The second discourse she identified is the "Ethical or Deferential Leadership" approach or what other scholars have referred to as a "Strategic Followership" policy.[36] This discourse recommends that South Korea should strive to be more in line with the international (DAC) norms which would mean increasing the amounts it distributes, raising the share of untied aid, and focusing on becoming a priority donor to select countries so that transactions costs in its projects are reduced.[37] This discourse on South Korean ODA policy has been developed and promoted by South Korea's Ministry of Foreign Affairs and Trade (MOFAT), and it has also been supported by the Korean International Cooperation Agency (KOICA) and various South Korean Non-Profit Organizations.[38]

While implementing either one of these discourses would lead to different patterns of ODA distributions, it is not so clear if they are different in terms of the Donor Interest or Recipient Needs dichotomy that was discussed above. In fact, practices representative of both discourses can contain characteristics of each of these models in that they are both designed to provide more effective aid to recipients, albeit in different ways, while, at the same time, promoting South Korea's international interests, both economically and politically. Despite these complexities, we can be clear about how South Korean ODA policies have changed over time. First, South Korea's ODA distributions had humble beginnings. According to OECD data, South Korea provided modest amounts of economic development assistance as early as 1985.[39] As the data in figure 4.5 indicate, these amounts remained low and relatively stable until the 1990s when they experienced moderate increases. Growth in South Korea's economic assistance continued throughout this decade, but these amounts experienced near exponential increases after the turn of the turn of the century. Such increases reflected the rapid and substantial progress South Korea had been making toward becoming an advanced industrial and democratic nation, a status it continues to enjoy today. Moreover, according to its first OECD Peer Review, South Korean officials pledged to numerous reforms, including raising aid levels and increasing the share of aid that is untied.[40]

As we can see from the above discussion, South Korea's ODA disbursements are the result of a complex interplay of international and domestic factors. Nonetheless, we know that South Korean officials wanted their nation to take a more active role in the design and implementation of ODA policy overall. As a DAC-member nation, however, this meant that South Korea had

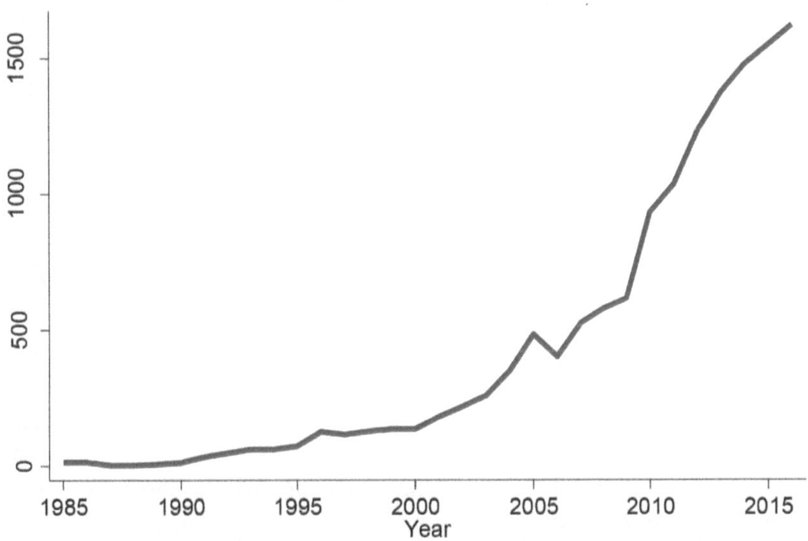

Figure 4.5. South Korea's Gross ODA Disbursements, 1985–2016.

to comply with evolving international development assistance norms, while at the same time protecting its domestic economic development concerns and promoting its international goals. To this end, South Korea's leaders have continually clarified their nation's approach to providing Official Development Assistance in a way that reflects its adherence to DAC recommendations but at the same time reflects their country's international and domestic interests. One way South Korea has balanced these competing interests is by emphasizing its own development experience and how this informs efforts to design aid that promotes balanced and sustainable growth.[41]

South Korean officials have increasingly emphasized that ODA programs not just promote shared economic growth for the populations within the nations that are recipients of its aid but also avoid exacerbating the economic disparities that very often plague development efforts in the world's least developed nations. Perhaps the most explicit articulation of these ODA principles is found in the "Seoul Development Consensus for Shared Growth," which was followed up with Korea's "Multi-Year Action Plan on Development." Both of these plans were announced at the G20 Summit held in Seoul in 2010, which attests to the efforts of South Korean officials to help make the economic assistance efforts of fellow DAC members more beneficial to recipient nations.[42] There are six core principles contained in the "Seoul

Development Consensus for Shared Growth," and these principles find their genesis in proposals introduced by Korean officials at two G20 summits, the 2009 summit in London and the one that followed in Toronto.[43] Once these principles and action items were adopted at the G20 Summit in Seoul in 2010, they have effectively replaced the principles that were embedded in what has been known as the Washington Consensus.[44]

The second document is the "Multi-Year Action Plan on Development" that listed one or more items to be implemented to accomplish development goals in nine target areas. These nine target areas are listed in this Plan, and South Korean officials offered both the previously mentioned six principles and nine implementation targets so that other recipient nations could have an improved development experience as aid recipients. In these documents, South Korea's ODA officials made it clear that balanced and sustainable development could occur only if ODA was distributed in a way that led to economic growth that was broadly shared among members of recipient countries' populations. This meant that DAC members would have to continually evaluate their aid disbursements to ensure that their ODA efforts truly led to growth that was "strong, sustainable, and balanced." On a more practical level, this led to recommendations that aid help increase aggregate demand in developing and, especially, low-income countries. This ODA goal was driven by the notion that such an outcome was possible only if donor nations worked harder to build relationships with aid recipients that were truly equitable.

While these policy documents reveal the efforts of South Korean leaders to influence ODA practices in a way that reflected its own development experience, there was a subsequent international agreement in which South Korea was heavily involved that reflects the parallel imperative of it being certain its own ODA practices adhere to international norms. The reference here is to the "Busan Partnership for Effective Development Cooperation" promulgated at the fourth High Level Forum on Aid Effectiveness held late in 2011 in South Korea.[45] While not antithetical to the principals and action items contained in the previous policy documents, the policies agreed to in the Busan Partnership are more comprehensive than those in the Seoul Development Consensus, and they required more reform action on the part of DAC-member nations. Such actions included encouraging increased donor-recipient cooperation, especially South–South and triangular cooperation efforts so that there can be more locally owned solutions to development problems that are contextually sensitive. In addition to a number of other recommendations, the Busan Partnership made policy changes that referred to providing finance to address the deleterious development impacts associated with climate change.[46]

There is little doubt that South Korea is committed to conducting its ODA disbursements in accordance with both the "Busan Partnership" and the "Seoul Consensus." Nonetheless, as former south Korean President, Lee Myung-Bak, noted in his New Year's speech, "[i]t is more difficult to give aid than to receive it."[47] President Lee's statement is clearly subject to interpretation, but it does tell us that South Korea remains committed to influencing the ODA policies of OECD nations in a way that continually make economic aid more and more effective. While this remarkable international achievement certainly required the continued application of diplomatic skill that South Korean leaders developed over the years of post-armistice period, becoming a member of the prestigious Development Assistance Committee (DAC) would not have been possible without this nation becoming this prosperous nation it had become.

NOTES

1. See e.g., Fukuyama (1992) for the classic statement of this idea.
2. These disputed islands are referred to as the Northern Territories and include the islands of Etorofu, Shilkotan, Habomai, and Kunashiri. Moreover, the ascendance of Vladimir Putin in Russia, and his Soviet-style approach to foreign relations has been interpreted by some as a return to Cold War politics.
3. Quoted in Heo and Roehrig (2014). Lee Myung-Bak was president of South Korea from 2008 to 2013.
4. The best illustration of this would be the Kwangju Incident. The City of Kwangju is in Southern Cholla province and the home town of former opposition leader and President, Kim Dae-Jung. From May 18 to 27 in 1980, citizens of the city rose up in protest of the Chun Doo-Hwan regime who established himself as president in a coup in the wake of Park Chung-Hee's assassination. Protests turned violent as citizens took up arms and looted police stations. Ultimately, regular units of the Korean Army moved into the city on May 27 and crushed the uprising in a brutal fashion. Disagreements remain over the number of casualties, but estimates range from two hundred to two thousand citizens and military.
5. Among the more oft-used measures are Freedom House's seven-point scale and Polity IV's authoritarian-democracy scale, which is based on such things as the autonomy of elected officials and the freedom of elections to the highest offices. It ranges from -10, most authoritarian, to +10, most democratic.
6. See Cummings (1981) who noted that People's Committees had formed governing groups in the South's various provinces but were suppressed by the occupying U.S. Army which replaced Japanese rule with a military government.
7. While straightforward on its face, this can be somewhat complicated because, while ODA can increase a recipient country's trade with the donor nation (direct impact), it can also lead to increased trade between the recipient and other nations (indirect impact).

8. Again, this would be groups whose members are the owners or intensive users of a nation's abundant factors.

9. Again, this would be groups whose members are the owners or intensive users of the nation's scarce factors. A good example would be Korean farmers, especially beef producers, who sought protection from U.S. beef exports during the period that the country's overall international trade was expanding.

10. It is true that some countries may contain socioeconomic groups that may neither be part of a government's support constituency nor potential challengers, which means that $PG + PCH < PT$. While this may be empirically accurate, the more important relationship rests not with the total political power in a country but rather the relative power of the government's supporters compared to that of potential challengers.

11. The subscript t refers to the time period before the expansion of diplomatic relations and $t+n$ refers to some time period after expanded diplomatic relations leads to more international trade.

12. See e.g., Kuznets (1977) and Amsden (1989).

13. See Reeve (1963).

14. On the obstacles that Korean workers faced in attempting to organize and form trade unions, see Amsden (1989).

15. Please note that the size of Korea's per capita GDP is indicated by the values on the Y-Axis on the right side of figure 4.3.

16. Between 1997 and 1998, the Korean Won lost nearly half its value vis-a-vis other currencies like the U.S. Dollar.

17. Again, please note that the values of Korea's total trade are shown on the left side of figure 4.4. This is important because while the total trade curve is below and to the right of the Per Capita GDP curve, it is much larger in value as the different scales on the left and right Y-axes make clear.

18. Like the previous figure, it is necessary to keep in mind the different scales of the two curves when examining the relationship between the two.

19. What is also important is that international trade became increasingly important in its contribution to Korea's GDP, growing from slightly over 15 percent of GDP in 1970 to just under 60 percent of GDP in 1995.

20. We discuss this in more detail below when we discuss South Korea's involvement in the G20 and the DAC of the OECD.

21. The table's data do not include the current president, Moon Jae-In, who took office in May of 2017.

22. This definition is from the OECD Glossary of Statistical Terms. See OECD (2017).

23. By DAC standards, a loan is concessional only if one-quarter of it is in the form of a grant. See Riddel (2008) for a discussion of ODA's history, characteristics, and effectiveness.

24. For a general discussion of ODA as one of many tools of economic statecraft that nations can employ, see Baldwin (1985).

25. South Korea joined OECD in 1996.

26. South Korea received ODA as late as 1995. It joined the DAC in 2010. See Bishwal (2011), OECD (2012), and Roehrig (2013). Japan received aid from the United States for a short time after the war, but it was not the economic-aid-dependent nation that South Korea was. For a detailed discussion, see Steinberg (1985) and Kim (2011). More general treatments can be found in Kuznets (1977), Amsden (1989), and Chung (2007).

27. Kim and Seddon (2005) discuss the diplomatic motivations behind South Korean ODA.

28. The classic work here is Johnson (1982). Amsden (1989) represents the application of this ides to South Korea.

29. See Newnham (2002) and Heo and Roehrig (2015) for discussions of South Korea's post-armistice isolation.

30. The most thorough discussion of the efforts of this topic is found in Heo and Roehrig (2014), which informs the discussion that follows.

31. The discussion that follows has benefitted from OECD (2012), Kim (2016) and Chung, Eom, and Jung (2016), and MOFAT (2012) the agency's Diplomatic Whitepaper.

32. See MOFAT (2012).

33. South Korea also provides technical assistance, which was the most important form of ODA in the early post-armistice period. It has declined as a share of South Korea's overall distributions in the last several years.

34. See Kim (2016).

35. The discussion that follows has benefitted by the findings in Sohn and Yoo (2015).

36. Kim (2016) examines the debates that occurred among ODA officials in South Korea.

37. Untied aid is that which does not require a recipient nation to purchase goods and services produced by the donor nation. See Chung, Eom, and Jung (2016), Kim, Kim, and Kim (2013), and Oh (2014) for a further discussion of these ideas.

38. Again, see Kim (2016).

39. Kim and Oh (2012) note that Korea first became effort as a donor was in 1963 when, in response to a USAID request, it provided technical training to selected recipients.

40. See OECD (2012) and Chun, Munyi, and Lee (2010).

41. On the interplay of these factors and the evolution of South Korea's ODA principles, see OECD (2012), Kim, Kim, and Kim (2013), and Kim (2016).

42. A discussion of the significance of the Seoul Development Consensus is provided in Kim (2010).

43. As suggested above, the fourth High Level Forum on Development Cooperation in 2011 was also an influential gathering.

44. The Washington Consensus has been the de facto guide for the economic assistance practices of DAC members since 1989. The approach in the Washington Consensus was essentially a neoclassical economics approach that, while widely criticized, had been in effect for two decades. See Birdsall et. al., (2010).

45. That this gathering was held in South Korea's southern peninsular port city of Busan is significant in and of itself. See www.busanhlf4.org.

46. Again, see www.busanhlf4.org.

47. Quoted in Kim (2010), p. 260. The full text of this speech can be accessed at the following website: http://www.ekoreannews.com/print_paper.php?number=3089&news_article.html.

Chapter Five

Diplomacy, Trade, and South Korea's Economic Development

When the Berlin Wall came down and the long period of icy relations between the democratic nations of the West and Asia and the communist nations of the Soviet bloc began to thaw, it was very clear that South Korea was a very different nation from the devastated country that emerged from the 1953 Armistice. Indeed, throughout the Cold War period, South Korea removed itself from international isolation, established formal relations with a growing number of nations throughout the world, and witnessed an explosive growth in its international trade. Moreover, throughout the same period, South Korea substantially reduced domestic poverty levels by achieving rapid economic growth, which put it on the path ultimately to having one of the largest economies in the world and being one of the globe's most prosperous nations.

To be sure, the Cold War years witnessed South Korea begin domestic and international transformations that would continue to the present day, and the remarkable story of this country's economic ascendance in particular has become an increasingly important topic of investigation for social scientists and Asia specialists.[1] The scholarly work that has been produced thus far has focused on how South Korean leaders formulated and implemented a set of domestic economic policies that expanded the country's trading relations, which in turn led to a period of rapid economic growth, allowing it to achieve its current level of prosperity and international influence. What this scholarship has not investigated, however, is how it was the diplomatic efforts of South Korea's post-armistice leaders to remove the nation from the international isolation it faced at the end of the Korean War that made the success of its domestic economic policies possible. Specifically, South Korea's international diplomatic and national economic successes were not two pillars of separate foreign and domestic policies but rather an interconnected set of factors that combined to form a single column that held up a unified national effort to elevate the country out of poverty, isolation, and dependence.

What this means is that the period of rapid economic growth would have been much less likely without the diplomatic successes South Korean leaders experienced early in the post-armistice period. This is because, without pulling South Korea out of international isolation and connecting itself with the nations of the world, international trade would not have expanded to the extent that it did. Consequently, if we do not investigate the relationship between the international diplomatic efforts and domestic economic policies implemented by South Korean leaders, we will not have a complete explanation for South Korea's post-armistice international rise. Our purpose in this chapter then is to connect the international successes of South Korea that we discussed in the previous chapters to its domestic economic development and make explicit how it was South Korea's diplomatic successes that not only directly elevated the country's international status but more importantly provided the necessary supportive international context for it to expand its exports and grow its domestic economy.

This will require the completion of several steps, the first of which involves a discussion of past scholarly efforts that show how diplomacy leads to an expansion of international trade between nations that establish and maintain formal diplomatic relations. We will then follow this discussion up with a specific examination of data on the South Korean case, revealing how it fits this general pattern. This analysis will be conducted for both the Cold War period as well as the current post-Cold War years so that we can show clearly that, even after South Korea experienced rapid economic growth and could employ more of its economic resources to support its leaders' efforts to become more influential internationally, diplomacy has remained an important factor in its ongoing rise to its currently influential middle-power status.

DIPLOMACY AND INTERNATIONAL TRADE

Establishing and maintaining formal diplomatic connections is a process that involves significant costs to the nation that seeks to engage in such relations. Rose (2007) has noted that the United States spent $42 billion in 2004 just on its diplomatic and consular missions, and he added that these are not only the costs associated with diplomatic efforts because the maintenance of embassies and consular offices requires other significant expenses such as providing security to all a nation's diplomatic and consular officials. Clearly, nations are willing to absorb these costs because establishing and maintaining diplomatic relations returns benefits to the sending nation. Specifically, formal relations allow nations to become connected to global affairs, elevating their respective standings among the nations of the world, and they also provide nations with the opportunity to obtain important information about the nations and regions in which they are engaged.

These are important benefits to be sure, but establishing and maintaining diplomatic formal relations is partner to another set of payoffs that is perhaps even more important. Existing research has shown that the diplomatic activities of nations also come with a variety of direct economic benefits. This is not surprising because nations that maintain formal diplomatic relations with many countries do not mask their motivations for such relations, which include economic goals such as promoting their respective nations' business interests. Rose (2007) pointed out that the U.S. Department of State has made explicit statements that make clear that such activities as "opening markets" and assisting U.S. businesses are among the activities in which embassy officials will engage. This is why the U.S. Department of Commerce, whose mission is among other things to promote U.S. business interests, work out of embassy and consular offices abroad.

The United States is not alone in being open about how officials stationed in its various embassies are actively involved in such things as market opening efforts in the promotion of their respective nations' business interests. Again, as Rose (2007) notes, the foreign ministries of the United Kingdom, Australia, Germany, and Canada have also made it clear that among their duties are promoting the interests of their respective countries' business firms.[2] Moreover, Ferguson and Froslid (2014) showed that officials in the Swedish Foreign Ministry also engage in business promotion activities and that their efforts have led to an expansion of Swedish exports to countries with which formal relations had been established.

That the establishment of an embassy leads to expanded trade with that country should not be surprising because the idea that nations have been successful using the tools of diplomacy for economic reasons, specifically, to establish and expand trading relations, has been well established in the international political economy literature. Pollins (1989a and 1989b) identified and measured how changes in "state-to-state diplomatic relations" affected trade flows between pairs of nations. The empirical connections that he identified were very strong, allowing him to conclude that diplomacy significantly boosted trade between nations with formally established diplomatic relations and that this was true even when controlling for all the standard economic factors that traditionally go into explaining levels of international trade between nations.

Pollins (1989a) referred to this as the "trade follows the flag" idea, and this finding has been expanded on by a number of different scholars who investigated the different tools of economic statecraft that nations employ to expand their trade with other nations. Among other things, these tools have included official state visits for trade and economic purposes as well as the creation of specific export promotion agencies, all of which lead to nations expanding overall trade with both existing and new trading partners.[3] Other expansions of this research have shown that the establishment of embassies leads to expansions of trade with countries by reducing entry costs for firms in countries with which formal relations have been established. Ferguson and Forslid (2014) note that the reduction of entry costs leads to increases in the extensive margins of trade, which typically benefit small and medium-sized firms that otherwise would not be able to overcome the entry costs associated with exporting to new markets. These authors' results were based on data from Sweden and Norway, and they confirmed earlier findings that the establishment of embassies also led to increases in the extensive margins of trade, where firms that are already exporting to countries with newly established diplomatic relations will increase their export volumes.

As we think about the case of South Korea and the expansion of its exports around the world, we must first note that diplomacy is not the only factor determining the direction and level of trade that occurs between pairs of nations. To be sure, the direction and level of trade that occurs between pairs of nations will depend on certain geopolitical factors, that is, whether or not a nation is a member of a free trade area or whether there is a common language between the traders such as the role played by the English language in the economic relations of the Commonwealth nations, or other languages shared by nations with a similar colonial past.[4] There will also be the impact of a nation belonging to a currency union, and perhaps the most important example would be that of Europe where transactions take place in Euros.[5] There is also distance, which affects the costs associated with moving goods and services across borders.

In addition to these factors, when considering the establishment of trading relations, there is no doubt that the nature of the goods to be exported or imported as well as their quality and price are also variables that need to be considered. However, such economic and product-specific factors are not the only ones that nations take into consideration when considering expansions of existing trade relations or when undertaking new trading partnerships. Nations entering into a trading relationship will want some assurance that they are establishing a connection with a country that will be economically reliable and politically stable in the long term. Having such assurances will minimize the country's economic risks and help guarantee that the interests of its business firms are protected. The best method to provide such assurances is to keep lines of communication open, and there is no better way for this to occur than to establish and maintain formal diplomatic relations.

This will be especially important in the case of South Korea, which we will show was among the most important factors behind its leaders' successful efforts to begin trading relations between itself and other nations as well as it increasing trade volumes where such relations already existed.[6] As we noted above, this is true not simply because leaders from Park Chung-Hee and after promoted the development and expansion of exports as crucial for the country's domestic economic development but more importantly because this export-led economic development strategy had to be preceded by a government effort to reconnect an internationally isolated South Korea with the rest of the world. Again, the Korean War left South Korea a poor, isolated, and utterly dependent nation, which meant that ending its isolation by rebuilding its international connections was a prerequisite for an export-led economic development strategy. Consequently the diplomatic efforts of post-armistice leaders to establish and maintain formal diplomatic relations with selected nations was a necessary first step in putting South Korea on the path to prosperity and international influence.

DIPLOMACY, TRADE, AND KOREAN ECONOMIC GROWTH DURING THE COLD WAR

As we have demonstrated in the previous chapter, it was not just that South Korea was diplomatically active during the Cold War years but more importantly that it was successful in its efforts to establish and maintain formal diplomatic connections with a growing number of nations. Such diplomatic successes are significant because the international system during the Cold War involved significant constraints on the foreign policy behavior of nations, especially those that were less powerful and dependent. Nonetheless, in spite of the narrowed options that South Korea's leaders had in their foreign policy choices earlier in the post-Armistice period, and also in spite of the fact that South Korea was still a poor nation that could offer little in terms of economic incentives for formal relations, this country's leaders were very successful at removing it from the international isolation that it faced in the early post-Armistice years. As we also discussed above, these diplomatic successes helped elevate South Korea internationally and, thus, were directly responsible for the improvements it experienced in its international status that we mapped in the preceding chapter. Our next task then is to connect these diplomatic successes to the positive domestic impacts that South Korea would come to experience once it implemented its export-led economic development policy.

This effort will involve exploring a number of empirical relationships, the first of which is the impact that South Korea's diplomatic achievements had on its international trade, especially, the growth in its exports that occurred throughout the last two decades of the Cold War. We recall that South Korea's first post-armistice president, Rhee Syngman, was initially successful at helping to reconnect his nation to the world. Indeed, he helped establish formal diplomatic relations between South Korea and a number of U.S. allies in Southeast Asia and West Europe. While his international successes were limited, they went well beyond his efforts to address the domestic economic needs of his country, which in many ways were an abject failure. This is mainly because he did not design and implement anything that resembled a rational domestic economic development strategy, and, in fact, he used the substantial amount of economic aid money he received from the United States to make up for deficits in his country's national budget and to purchase consumption goods. This is why South Korea was still in a condition of economic distress when Rhee was forced to leave office in 1960.

In addition to using the tools of diplomacy to build formal connections with as many nations as possible both to elevate South Korea's international position and to outpace the diplomatic efforts of Pyongyang, Park Chung-Hee designed and implemented what has been touted as a model of economic development that can be emulated by the world's developing nations.[7] This economic development strategy is referred to as an export-led approach to promoting economic growth, and it involved providing incentives for certain domestic producers that were selected for favorable treatment to reorient themselves as exporters of South Korean products. The favorable treatment they received involved South Korean leaders rationing the country's limited capital to these selected producers in various forms like loans on very favorable terms and, in some cases, direct subsidies.

While scholars have offered in-depth discussions of the details of President Park's export-led economic development strategy from the domestic side of the equation, they have not touched on the international side of his policy to promote the economic development of South Korea. As a result, existing scholarly treatments of South Korea's economic development policies have not explained to which nations an isolated and poor South Korea would send its exports. In other words, South Korea's efforts to remove itself from the state of international isolation heaped upon it after the Korean War is taken for granted, which means that the first empirical relationship we examine is that between leaders' efforts to use the tools of diplomacy to establish and maintain formal relations with selected nations and the promotion of South

Korean trade. To determine if this relationship holds up in post-armistice South Korea, that is, if the expansion of trade did in fact follow the South Korean flag, we compare trends in South Korea's progress in establishing diplomatic relations with the expansion of its international trade.

The data in figure 5.1 contain parallel plots of growth in South Korea's formal diplomatic connections and increases in its international trade. We noted in previous sections that, from the promulgation of the armistice ending the Korean War to the formal end of the Cold War in Europe in 1989, South Korea's diplomatic connections had grown by over 3000 percent. Indeed, by 1989, this dramatic increase in diplomatic connections amounted to nearly 90 percent of all the diplomatic relations South Korea would end up with to this very day. What we can observe immediately from the data in the figure is that South Korea's international trade grew dramatically throughout this time and this growth paralleled the success South Korean leaders in establishing and maintaining formal diplomatic relations. Growth in South Korean trade outpaced the country's increase in diplomatic connections in the immediate aftermath of the armistice, but, over the next three decades, they both grew nearly in tandem. We take a closer look at these parallel developments.

We see from the figure that, in the immediate aftermath of the Korean War, South Korea's trade levels were virtually nonexistent, and they then jumped

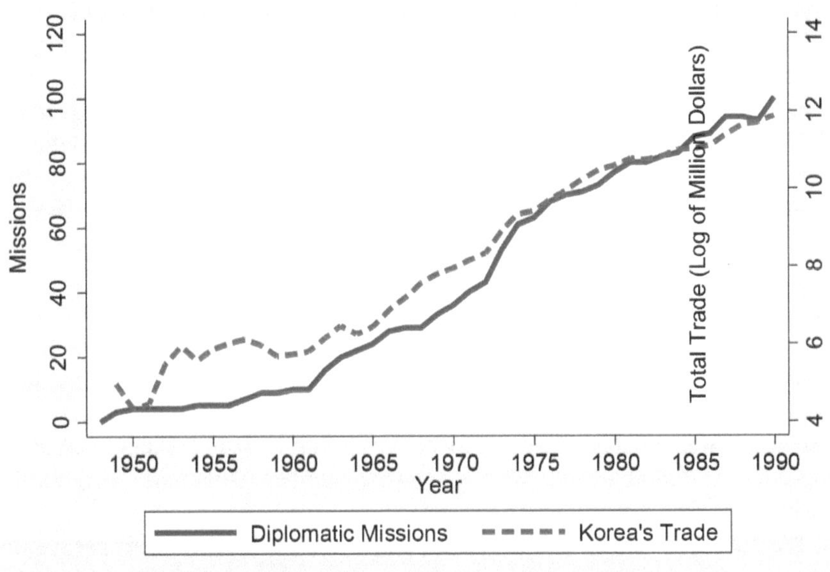

Figure 5.1. Diplomatic Missions and Trade in Korea, 1948–1990.

significantly when peace was restored on the peninsula and the government in Seoul was able to restart its domestic and international economic activities. Unfortunately, the latter half of the 1950s was a turbulent time in South Korean domestic politics, and the data in figure 5.1 indicate that both trade levels and diplomatic successes remained relatively flat. South Korea's international trade even dipped near the end of the decade when domestic unrest had increased to such levels that president Rhee was forced to resign. The replacement of Rhee Syngman did not lead to a calming of domestic political tensions as unrest continued until a military coup put General Park Chung-Hee in power in 1960. This proved to be a pivotal event in the domestic and international affairs of South Korea.

The data in figure 5.1 indicate, the ascension of Park Chung-Hee to power began a period of diplomatic success and trade expansion that would in many ways continue into the post-Cold War period. Indeed, the data make clear that a continued increase in levels of South Korean trade moved in tandem with the President and his successors' ongoing successes in establishing and maintaining formal diplomatic relations with a growing number of nations throughout the world during the Cold War and beyond. Specifically, in 1960, Korea's total international trade was just over $300 million, but, ten years later, it had grown by over 900 percent to over $2.8 billion. In the next decade, Korea's total trade grew even faster—over 1000 percent—to $40 billion, and, in the next two decades, South Korea's total international trade continued to grow but at somewhat lower rates. In the 1980s, total trade grew by over 300 percent, and, between 1990 and 2000, growth dropped to just over 200 percent.

Having established in the data that the expansion of South Korean trade followed the establishment and maintenance of formal diplomatic relations, it is next incumbent on us to demonstrate that the expansion of South Korean trade throughout the Cold War was partner to an increase in domestic economic benefits. Specifically, we will need to present data that indicates how it was that the expansion of trade that led to an increase in the country's level of economic development, reducing its initially substantial levels of poverty. This is because making the connection between international trade and per capita gross domestic product will solidify the argument that Seoul's export-led economic development strategy produced the positive results it did because it was proceeded by the success of South Korean leaders to connect the country diplomatically with a growing number of nations, particularly early in the post-armistice period.

We showed in the previous chapters how South Korea's GDP per capita grew substantially as the Cold War period progressed. Indeed, from 1961 to 1979, the period of the Park Chung-Hee presidency, per capita GDP in South Korea had increased by almost 200 percent. Moreover, from the time of President Park's assassination in 1979 to the end of the Cold War in Europe in 1989, per capita GDP in South Korea was two and one-quarter times larger. What is most relevant about this growth for our purposes is not simply that the pattern that South Korea's per capita GDP revealed from the mid-1950s to the end of the Cold War, but rather that, in the post-armistice period, international trade and indicators of domestic economic development grew in tandem, accelerating over time.

That growth in South Korea's international trade preceded that of the country's GDP and per capita GDP suggests that the former certainly contributed to the latter. As revealed in figure 5.2,[8] it is growth in South Korea's international trade that ultimately pulled along increments in its GDP per capita, and, thus, this relationship holds up statistically even when we test it in a statistical model at one- and five-year lags.[9] This relationship is equally strong when we pair growth in total international trade with gross national income (figure 5.3).[10] This is an excellent indicator of South Korea's overall prosperity, and the data in the figure are clear that its relationship is similar to that of per capita GDP. Specifically, these two are strongly correlated, and, like the case of per capita GDP, this remains true at one- and five-year time lags as well as others.[11]

While our presentation in graphic form of trends in trade expansion and per capita gross domestic product and then trade expansion and gross national

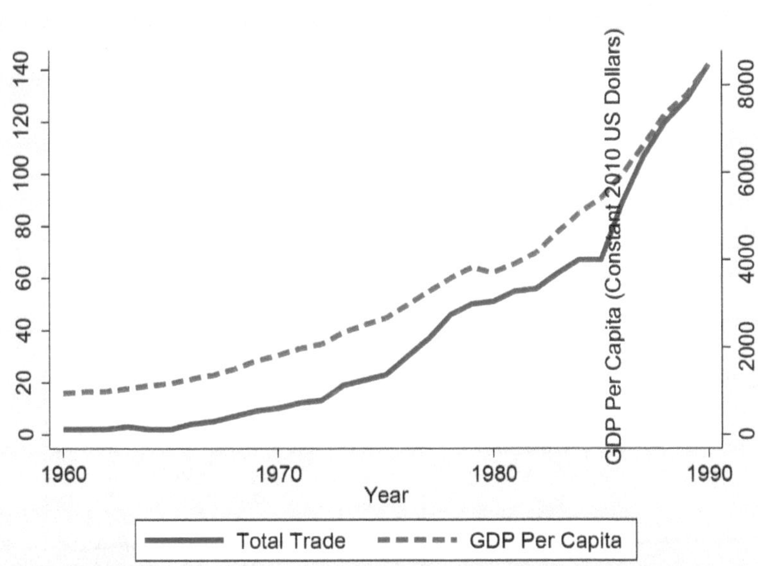

Figure 5.2. The Relationship between Trade and Per Capita GDP in Korea.

income reveal that these two pairs of phenomena did increase in tandem, we need to take another step in our analysis to confirm more thoroughly what the data in these graphs have uncovered. Specifically, we will need to conduct a statistical analysis that will allow us to estimate the extent to which the establishment and maintenance of formal diplomatic relations led to the expansion of South Korean trade, thus allowing for the successful implementation of its domestic economic development strategy. This effort begins with us specifying the variable to be explained: the level of trade between South Korea and other nations. These levels of trade will be defined as international dyads and will be calculated by combining the values of South Korea's imports and exports to a partner country for each year covered by the series. This value is entered into our model for estimation as the natural log of this sum. Data on the dollar value of exports and imports between South Korea and other nations are obtained from the Correlates of War (COW) project available at the following website: http://www.correlatesofwar.org/.

As we have noted above, there are many factors that affect the level of trade between pairs of nations, but our principal concern here is the extent to which South Korean trade grew throughout the Cold War years because South Korean leaders were successful at establishing and maintaining formal diplomatic relations. To measure whether or not a bilateral diplomatic relationship exists, we use South Korea's establishment and continuation

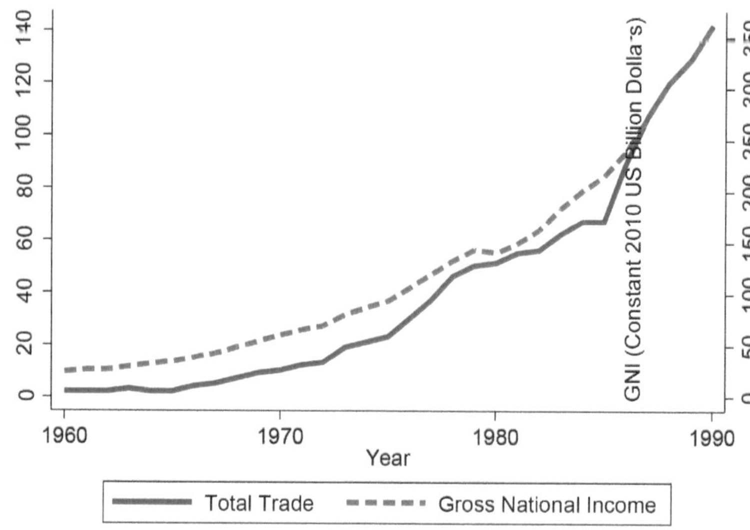

Figure 5.3. Trade and Gross National Income in Korea.

of embassy in a partner country as our indicator. If South Korea established and maintained an embassy in a nation, that dyad is coded 1 for each year for which that embassy was maintained. All other years are coded a 0 in that dyad.[12] We expect that South Korea will establish an embassy in a nation as a signal that is it confident that the two nations will maintain stable political and prosperous economic relations in the long term. As a result, our expectation is that dyads coded a 1 will manifest higher levels of bilateral trade with South Korea than those that are not.

We will also need to include other political, economic, and geographic factors in our analysis that existing studies have shown affect the level of trade that exists between pairs of nations. Perhaps the most important are economic factors, particularly the level of economic development, both of South Korea and of its potential trading partners. We measure South Korea's level of economic development as per capita GDP, which is entered into the models we estimate below as the natural log of that value.[13] Including South Korea's per capita GDP is important because it serves as a control variable to ensure that we get a proper estimate of the impact of diplomatic relations on its trade. Moreover including this variable will also allow us to track the impact of South Korea's per capita GDP on its trade levels as its economy grows. Our assumption is that the impact of GDP in increasing South Korean trade levels will grow as the size of its GDP increases. This is important because it means that GDP will be more important later in the Cold War period than earlier and in the post-Cold War period than during the Cold War years.[14]

Concerning the impact of a trading partner's per capita GDP, we expect this overall relationship to be positive and significant. There are two reasons for this, the first of which concerns the fact that South Korea's initial trading relations in the Cold War years were with nations that were at much higher levels of economic development. The second reason for this is our expectation that South Korean trade will grow with a nation in a dyad as the size of the nation's GDP increases as well. That South Korea exported more goods as the post-armistice period progressed has been clearly revealed in the data presented above. Parallel with this is our expectation that nations in a dyad will increase their trade with South Korea as their respective economies grow. This economic growth will be partner to increased demand for more goods, and it will also help trading partners to earn more foreign exchange, which will enable them to import the growing amount of goods that South Korea would come increasingly to export.

While the size of an importing nation's economy is a measure of its potential economic importance, we also wanted to be certain that we controlled for other ways that potential trading partners would be likely to begin economic exchanges with South Korea. We measure this potential in two different ways. First, we include the measure of a potential trading partner's geographic distance from South Korea. The idea is simply that distance should be inversely proportional to the level of trade that exists between South Korea and another country.[15] We also measured a country's potential to trade with South Korea as that country's level of democracy. We used two different indicators to capture a nation's level of democracy changed. The first is Polity IV data, which is more an indicator of a nation's democratic institutions and processes, and the second is the Freedom House Index, which is less about government institutions and more tuned in to levels of individual freedom in different countries.

Our expectation is that a country's level of democracy should be, ceteris paribus, positively related to the amount that it trades with South Korea. The most important reason for this is simply that South Korea's initial diplomatic contacts and, thus, trading partners during the early years of the post-armistice period were the United States and, as time went on, Japan and other democratic nations. Moreover, for the entire period of the Cold War, South Korea had very limited economic contacts with nations that had communist governments and virtually no formal diplomatic relations. For these reasons, we expect a nation's level of democracy should be positively related to the amount that it trades with South Korea.[16]

Finally, we included the natural log of South Korea's population as well as that of all other potential trading partners. We certainly expect there to be a positive relationship between the size of South Korea's population and the amount it trades in general, and we also expect that this relationship will be positive with respect to the population of other nations, albeit somewhat weaker. Although certainly influenced by the size and structure of a nation's economy, larger populations translate into higher levels of demand for goods and services as well as a larger potential to contribute to a growing supply of goods and services. On the other hand, we expect this impact to be weaker in the Cold War period—compared to post-Cold War years—because while there have been potential trading partners with South Korea that have very large populations like the United States, there were also nations with large populations with which South Korea had little or no trade, at least until much later in the Cold War period.[17] In addition to this, there were also other nations with smaller populations that have evolved significant trading relations with South Korea throughout the Cold War.[18]

With our dependent variable defined and those factors that will determine the level of trade between South Korea and other dyads specified, we note that the model for specification is as follows:

$$Y_i = a + \beta_1 X_i^1 + \ldots + \beta_K X_i^K + e_i \quad i = 3{,}383 \tag{1}$$

where Y_{it} is a continuously valued, unobserved variable estimating the logged volume of trade that exists in a dyad in a particular year for the period under consideration, and $X_i^{I.K}$ is a one by eight vector containing the covariates. From the above discussion, recall that the covariate of interest (1) is a dummy variable indicating whether a partner nation in a dyad has a formal diplomatic relationship with South Korea in a particular year for the period under consideration. Five of the covariates are continuous variables, capturing (2) the size of South Korea's GDP in a year for the period under consideration, (3) the size of a dyad's GDP for a year throughout the period under consideration, (4) the geographic distance between South Korea and a dyad, (5) South Korea's population, and (6) the population of a dyad. The final two variables (7 and 8) are discrete variables, capturing the level of political freedom and democracy of a trading partner in a dyad.[19]

We know that the data we use to explain the level of trade South Korea will have with a country in a dyad will involve significant heteroscedasticity, and, as a result, we must address this in our estimation of the above model. One method involves using heteroscedasticity-robust statistics after estimating the model with Ordinary Least Squares (OLS).[20] This is the recommended method but using the Generalized Least Squares method we ultimately use can lead to problems in the panel-specific AR(1) process and, thus, overconfidence in our estimates. We did estimate our models with OLS using Panel-Corrected Standard Errors, and some differences did exist in some of our coefficients but not on our principal variable of interest.[21] Moreover, this estimation method is more efficient when one knows the form that heteroscedasticity takes, and since we are not sure of the exact form the heteroscedasticity will take in our models, we modeled its form using an estimation technique that produces more efficient results. Specifically, we began by specifying the form of the heteroscedasticity and then by estimating our models model using Weighted Least Squares. The specific method we use is known as Feasible Generalized Least Squares (FGLS), and it will allow us to generate the best estimate of the impact that the factors in our model will have on the level of trade between South Korea and a nation in a dyad.[22]

The results of estimating models using this procedure are presented in table 5.1, and we first note that the coefficient estimates in the table were obtainable by using the FGLS method noted above, which produces estimates by panel-specific AR (1) (the first-order autoregressive) process and heteroskedastic but uncorrelated error structures. We estimate our parameters using three slightly different models because we expect there to be a strong relationship between our two measures of a nation's level of democracy, the Polity IV measure, and the Freedom House measure. Specifically, our first model does not contain either of these measures while Model 2 contains the

Freedom House measure and Model 3 contains the Polity IV indicator of a nation's level of democracy.

The results presented in table 5.1 indicate that, except for conflicting values on the Polity IV and Freedom House indicators, the explanatory variables we included in our models are statistically significant and the sizes and signs of the estimated parameters are consistent across all three models. Concerning our principal variable of interest, results in the table tell us that it is positive and statistically significant in all three models. This variable is defined by South Korea's establishment and maintenance of an embassy in a partner country, and parameter estimates tell us clearly that our theoretical argument is correct in that the establishment and maintenance of an embassy in a dyad is associated with higher volumes of trade with that country. This finding is consistent with the well-established finding that "trade follows the flag,"[23] and it is also consistent with the arguments in Rose (2007) that nations absorb the costs of establishing and maintaining diplomatic relations for the economic benefits that are partner to these formal relations.

These results are particularly important in the South Korean case not simply because the establishment and maintenance of formal diplomatic relations between South Korea and other nations resulted in higher volumes of trade. They are also important for several other reasons. Specifically, the higher

Table 5.1. Dyadic Trade between South Korea and Partner Countries (1960–1990)

	Model 1	*Model 2*	*Model 3*
Diplomatic Tie$_{t-1}$	0.491***	0.651***	0.456***
	(0.059)	(0.070)	(0.061)
*ln*Korea GDP$_{t-1}$	0.310***	0.225**	0.329***
	(0.041)	(0.070)	(0.039)
*ln*Partner GDP$_{t-1}$	1.044***	1.023***	0.926***
	(0.024)	(0.026)	(0.032)
Partner's Level of Democracy$_{t-1}$	—	—	0.034***
			(0.005)
Partner's Freedom House Index$_{t-1}$	—	–0.118***	—
		(0.019)	
*ln*Distance	–0.933***	–1.007***	–0.848***
	(0.091)	(0.091)	(0.078)
*ln*Korea Population$_{t-1}$	3.176***	4.717***	3.644***
	(0.418)	(0.935)	(0.396)
*ln*Partner Population$_{t-1}$	–0.268***	–0.215***	–0.214***
	(0.032)	(0.027)	(0.043)
Constant	–34.052***	–48.680***	–39.298***
	(4.172)	(9.307)	(3.918)
No. of Obs.	3383	2290	3172
No. of Countries	147	146	132

volumes of trade that diplomatic relations led to also became a key factor in helping South Korean leaders remove their country from international isolation during the Cold War years. Indeed, nations that were good candidates for formal diplomatic relations were also good candidates for South Korea and its businesses to build economic relationships, which became characterized by growing amounts of trade during the years of the Cold War. In addition to this, growing trade volumes that resulted from establishing and maintaining diplomatic relations allowed South Korea to be successful implementing a its export-led development strategy, allowing the country ultimately to become the prosperous and influential nation it is today.

We showed that the influence of diplomatic relations on increasing international trade held up even controlling for other factors that the scholarly literature has shown are associated with levels of international trade. What our findings also indicate is that the size of the South Korean economy was also an important factor in this relationship. Indeed, results in table 5.1 tell us that trade in a dyad increased as did the size of the South Korean economy measured as the natural log of its gross domestic product as a one-year lag. We also see from the data in the table that the size of a trading partner's economy is also positive and statistically significant and that it carried a much larger impact than the size of the South Korean economy. This difference reflects the fact that South Korea's GDP was smaller on average than the economies of those countries with which it traded in the Cold War period.

We expected the impact of diplomacy and a trading partner's economy to be both positive and significant, but we were somewhat surprised that South Korean GDP was as important as it proved to be in our results. Indeed, while its positive impact was one-third of that of a trading partner's GDP, the size of South Korea's GDP was a very important factor in the growth of its international trade throughout the years of the Cold War. These results are indicative of the idea that domestic, economic, and international political factors worked together to boost the level of trade in which South Korea engaged throughout the years of the Cold War. What was perhaps more surprising in our results is the differential impact that democracy and political freedom had on South Korean trade, depending on how these concepts were measured in our models.

Specifically, while the coefficients on both measures were statistically significant, the Polity IV measure produced a small but positive and statistically significant coefficient in Model 3, but the Freedom House Index in Model 2 resulted in a small but negative impact. These conflicting results are due to these two measures picking up on different aspects of a nation's freedom and democracy. The Polity IV measure reflects the fact that from early on in the post-armistice period, South Korea's principal trading partners were democratic countries like the United States, Japan, and the nations of West Europe, which is why its impact was positive and statistically significant even if small. The Freedom House Index, on the other hand, is more sensitive to whether a nation's population is reflective of political freedom or not. As a result, these results are indicative more of the set of nations with which South Korea did not trade. In other words, nations that were not democratic but were experiencing some elevation in their political freedom were less likely to be part of South Korean trading relations during the Cold War years.

As we also expected, the impact of a trading partner's distance from South Korea was statistically significant and possessed the expected positive sign. In all three of our models, the distance of a nation from South Korea was negatively related to the level of trade between them. This is a finding that confirms the expected impact of geography, but, in the South Korean case, it also reflects the fact that a good part of South Korea's trade portfolio in the years of the Cold War manifested a regional bias. Specifically, with the exception of the United States and its NATO-nation allies, South Korean trade reflected a preference for the nations of East and Southeast Asia.

Finally, there is the relationship between trade and the population of both South Korea and its trading partners. As expected, the natural log of South Korea's population revealed a positive and statistically significant relationship with the level of trade it conducted with other nations.[24] This was an expected finding because the size of a nation's population is positively related to the volume of its international trade. The coefficient on a trading partner's population was also statistically significant but negative and carried a very small impact. This very small impact was most likely due to the fact that, with the United States as the principal exception, throughout the period of the Cold War, South Korea did not share as much trade with countries that possessed the largest populations in the world. These include countries like the People's Republic of China and the Soviet Union.

The findings presented thus far are clear that, throughout the Cold War years, the levels of international trade in which South Korea engaged were higher with nations with which it had established and maintained formal diplomatic relations. While this confirms a finding that is well established in the scholarly literature, calibrating this relationship for the South Korean case is important for another reason, one related to how scholars have explained South Korea's rise to its current position of international influence. In the wake of the Korean War, South Korea was a poor, dependent, and internationally isolated nation, but today it is a truly prosperous and influential international actor. Most explanations for this dramatic transformation have focused on the rapid economic growth that South Korea experienced. Our results make clear that the size of South Korea's GDP was contributory, but it was not the factor that put South Korea in the path to international influence.

Indeed, for South Korea to implement its export-led economic development strategy—which helped spark its rapid economic development—it was essential for it to reconnect with the nations of the world from which it was isolated after the Korean War. Consequently, it was the efforts of early post-armistice presidents, especially Park Chung-Hee, who began the process, but also successors like Chun Doo-Hwan and Roh Tae-Woo, who used to tools of diplomacy to continue to expand South Korea's formal diplomatic connections with the nations of the world. The success of these international efforts helped pave the way for its international trade to grow, leading ultimately to South Korea's rapid economic growth and the prosperity and influence it currently enjoys. What is most important is that South Korea's diplomatic successes in the Cold War years helped start its international rise at a time when it was still a poor country.

DIPLOMACY, TRADE, AND ECONOMIC GROWTH IN THE POST-COLD WAR PERIOD

We have shown above that South Korea's leaders put their country on the path to international influence by their successful diplomatic efforts early in the post-Armistice period. Indeed, it was during the years of the Cold War that South Korean presidents used the diplomatic resources they had at their disposal to connect their once isolated and poor country to a growing number of nations throughout the world. Although a rigid Cold War alliance system limited the number of nations that were available for formal relations, these initial diplomatic successes provided South Korea's leaders with an increasingly supportive international context and allowed them to employ the export promotion tools President Park put together as part of the country's domestic economic development strategy. This is how South Korea, at a time when it was without an abundance of economic resources and was, at the same time, pulling itself out of international isolation, managed to help its businesses begin exporting, increasingly expanding South Korea's level of international trade.

The importance of diplomacy was either understated or missing in existing but otherwise important explanations for South Korea's rapid economic development and ultimate rise to international influence. Consequently, our giving them the weight they deserve has allowed us to provide a more complete picture of the story of South Korea's international rise. While the empirical results presented above have made clear how important diplomacy was in helping put South Korea on the path to its current position of international influence before it was the prosperous nation it is today, they did not in any way indicate that South Korea's economic growth and its continually expanding economy were unimportant in its international rise. In fact, results for the Cold War years showed that South Korea's economic growth also helps account for the country's rise to middle-power status and it contributed to its rise in both direct and indirect ways.

Economic growth has been directly important to South Korea's international rise, especially in more recent years, because it would not have been able to join and then influence the international organizations in which it has memberships without rapid growth providing it with the high level of economic wherewithal it currently possesses. As we discussed above, in 2010, South Korea became a member of the Development Assistance Committee (DAC) of the OECD, the world's most important governing body for the distribution of Official Development Assistance. We also showed that, as with its participation in other international organizations like the G20 and APEC, South Korea did not simply join OECD's Development Assistance Committee, it used its membership to influence the direction of Official Development Assistance (ODA) policy in a way that would, in the view of South Korea's ODA leaders, render it more effective and, thus, beneficial to recipient nations. Again, this would not have been possible unless South Korea had experienced the rapid economic growth that its domestic development strategy helped encourage, ultimately leading it to become the prosperous country it is today.

South Korea's economic growth was indirectly important to its rise to international influence because it continued to work side by side with the ongoing diplomatic efforts of its leaders in the post-Cold War years to accelerate its rise to international influence. The data in figure 5.4 indicate that, like the years of the Cold War, both South Korea's international trade and diplomatic missions continued to increase after the Berlin Wall fell in the wake of the Cold War's end. While diplomacy did experience a dip in the latter part of the 1990s because the currency crisis that South Korea and other Asian nations suffered during these years required some international adjustments, South Korea's diplomatic efforts recovered and continued on an upward trajectory until the present day. International trade, on the other hand, continued to grow throughout this period, albeit not in an entirely monotonic fashion.

We see from the data in figure 5.5 that South Korea's overall trade levels did contract somewhat during the Won crisis of 1997, and they also experienced a contraction later in the first decade of the twenty-first century. The latter contraction was due to the financial crisis of 2008, which was followed by the most severe recession the world's developed and developing countries

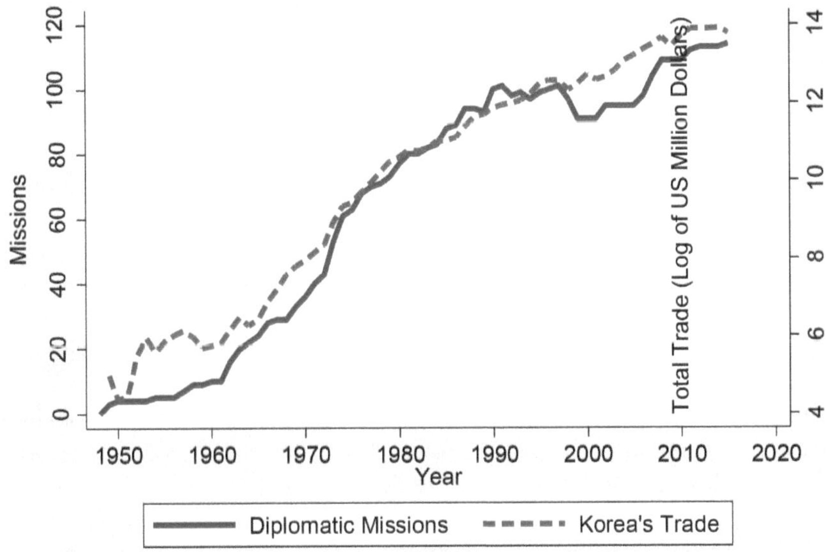

Figure 5.4. Diplomatic Missions and International trade, 1948–2015.

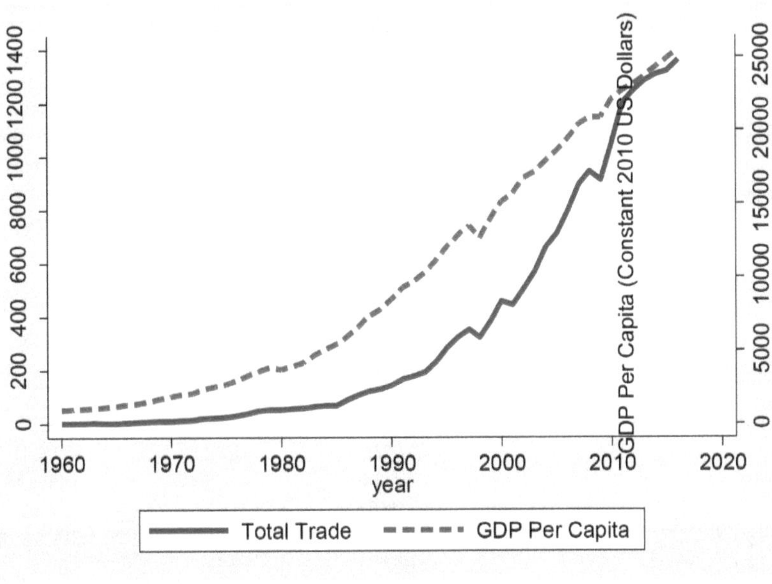

Figure 5.5. Relationship Between Trade and Per Capita GDP in Korea, 1960–2015.

experienced since the Great Depression. The data in the figure also reveal a more recent dip in South Korea's international trade level. Nonetheless, in spite of these dynamics in the overall levels of South Korean international trade, this country's GDP continued to experience increases throughout the entire post-Cold War period. The one exception is a contraction in GDP growth that took place during the Won crisis at the end of the 1990s. However, we see from the data in figure 5.5 that the country's economic growth recovered rather quickly and then continued on its upward trajectory.

Since the empirical results presented above indicated that both the diplomatic efforts of South Korean leaders and the country's GDP contributed to its international rise during the Cold War years—again, a period of time when South Korea was still a poor country—we maintain the expectation that these two sets of factors would continue to work together throughout the post-Cold War years, particularly as South Korean leaders enjoyed an expanding amount of economic wherewithal to employ in their foreign policy efforts. To make this determination in a more definitive manner, we will provide a follow-up empirical analysis where we map the impact of the same factors on South Korean trade levels but only for the years of the post-Cold War period. The results of performing this follow-up analysis are presented in table 5.2.

Table 5.2. Dyad Trade between South Korea and Partner Countries (1991–2015)

	Model 1	*Model 2*	*Model 3*
Diplomatic Tie_{t-1}	0.750***	0.755***	0.704***
	(0.055)	(0.055)	(0.059)
*ln*Korea GDP_{t-1}	0.148***	0.149***	0.142**
	(0.045)	(0.045)	(0.046)
*ln*Partner GDP_{t-1}	0.970***	0.956***	0.977***
	(0.017)	(0.018)	(0.018)
Partner's Level of $Democracy_{t-1}$	—	—	–0.000
			(0.004)
Partner's Freedom House $Index_{t-1}$	—	–0.025*	—
		(0.013)	
*Ln*Distance	-0.715***	–0.743***	–0.766***
	(0.055)	(0.054)	(0.058)
*ln*Korea $Population_{t-1}$	4.101***	4.115***	4.214***
	(0.588)	(0.581)	(0.600)
*ln*Partner $Population_{t-1}$	–0.063**	–0.046*	–0.076**
	(0.019)	(0.022)	(0.024)
Constant	–44.800***	–44.642***	–45.398***
	(5.938)	(5.861)	(6.056)
No. of Obs.	4375	4375	3841
No. of Countries	185	185	162
chi2	12226.48	13443.78	10341.48

Significance Level: * $p<0.05$, ** $p<0.01$, *** $p<0.001$.

In examining our results, we are naturally interested in determining if, in these more recent data, diplomacy continued to have the substantively important impact on levels of trade in South Korean dyads, and we are also interested in determining if the influence of the South Korean economy on dyadic trade changed. We will then compare these results across these two periods of time, which will allow us to track any differences that may have occurred in the statistical significance of our two variables of interest as well as our controls. In addition to this, we will also be able to observe any changes that occur in the direction and size of the coefficients on diplomacy and the South Korean economy while controlling for the impact of the factors we included in the analysis of data for the Cold War years.

The format of the follow-up analysis we conducted for the post-Cold War period mirrored that conducted for the years of the Cold War. Specifically, the structure of the models, the method of estimation, and the explanatory and control variables that were included were all the same, and an initial inspection of the coefficients presented in table 5.2 reflects a strong similarity with those produced for the Cold War years of 1960 to 1990. The coefficients for the variables on South Korea's diplomatic connections and the size of its Gross Domestic Product were both statistically significant with signs in the same direction. These results indicated that both of our factors of primary interest continued to work together in the post-Cold War period, maintaining their influence in elevating South Korea's rise to international influence. The weights associated with the sizes of these two factors' impacts, however, were different across the Cold War and post-Cold War samples.

Because South Korea was still a poor country during the Cold War period, its leaders had little economic wherewithal at their disposal to assist in achieving the country's foreign policy goals. As a result, we thought that diplomacy would possibly have a larger impact in the early post-Armistice years than after the Cold War ended when the South Korean economy had grown and became more of a factor in assisting its leaders to achieve international goals. Coincident with this, we also thought that the size of South Korea's GDP would be larger in the later period of time, since it was after the Cold War that leaders employed South Korea's increasing wealth to directly influence its ability to join a number of important international organizations and, thus, accelerate its international rise. Results in table 5.2, however, indicate just the opposite impact as the coefficient on South Korean diplomacy was larger in the post-Cold War years when it had already entered into its rapid growth period, and the direct impact of South Korean GDP was lower at this time than when the country was still relatively poor during the Cold War.

What these results tell us is that both international political (diplomatic) and domestic and international economic factors worked together to increase South Korea's levels of international trade, and, as a result, domestic wealth, which together helped it continue on the path to becoming an influential middle power. These are important results that we do not want to understate because it forms the basis on which we will explain South Korea's international status and how it changed throughout both the Cold War and post-Cold War periods as well as its current and future responses to the challenges it faces in East Asia today. Nonetheless, while the difference in the relative impacts of these two factors across the two periods of our analysis were not dramatically different, they do require that we rethink our initial expectations about the levels of their impacts in the two sets of data we examined. Our revised interpretation of these differences proceed from what we refer to as a supply argument, that is, assessing impacts based on the supply or availability of economic wherewithal as well as possible new diplomatic connections.

Many of the initial diplomatic connections South Korea's leaders secured in the Cold War years were with nations that were clearly in the U.S./NATO side of the international divide at this time. Thus, even though South Korea's leaders did have to contend with constraints on the foreign policy choices at this time, making connections with the United States's NATO allies was relatively easy. In the post-Cold War period, however, South Korea faced a dwindling supply of potential diplomatic partners and many of those that were available were formerly part of the block of communist nations. Consequently, when leaders in Seoul approached these nations, establishing formal connections was not automatic and involved more diplomatic effort than those of the previous period. It is for this reason that the coefficient on diplomacy was most likely higher in the post-Cold War period than that which preceded it.

The size of the South Korean GDP and the economic wherewithal it provided to the country's leaders worked in pretty much the same way. In the Cold War period, available economic resources were at a minimum and, thus, had to be employed for foreign policy purposes with great care. In the later period, on the other hand, South Korea had entered the period of rapid economic growth and enjoyed an increasingly large economy that provided higher levels of prosperity to the people of that nation. Given this large differential in the supply of available economic wherewithal for the achievement of international goals, the coefficient on the size of the South Korean GDP should have been larger in the earlier period than after the demise of the Berlin Wall when economic resources were much more plentiful for these purposes.

There were other differences in the sizes of coefficients between the two periods of time we examined, and, although these differences do not change our overall interpretation of the results our analysis produced, they are worthy of mention. First, our two measures of a nation's level of democracy and freedom, while different depending on which measure we examine, were statistically significant in the earlier sample, but, in the post-Cold War analysis, they were not. This result suggests that the supply of potential diplomatic partners in the post-Cold War years involves more nations that registered lower scores on both measures of freedom and democracy.

In addition to this, the distance of a potential trading partner from South Korea remained negative in the post-Cold War data, but its impact was smaller than during the Cold War years. This result was most likely due to the manner in which transportation technology and e-commerce had made the world smaller, enhancing the ability of nations like South Korea to engage in international trade with nations that were increasingly distant from Seoul. The same is true for the coefficients on a trading partner's population and the size of a trading partner's economy. What these values tell us is that, as the South Korean economy grew and the products and services it produced became more diversified, its import and export mixes also became more diversified, albeit with a growing share of finished goods that were higher in their capital and technology contents. These changes in South Korea's trade portfolio rendered such factors less important for a nation to be a member of a South Korean trading dyad.

NOTES

1. See chapter 2 for a discussion of the scholarly literature produced on this topic.
2. See Rose (2007) for specific quotes from the foreign offices of Canada, the United Kingdom, Germany, and Australia on how they are promoting the business interests of their respective nations.
3. See Nitsch (2007) and Lederman et. al., (2010).
4. An example here would be the French language and trade between France and its former African colonies.
5. There are many other currency unions such as that defined by the East Caribbean Dollar and two Franc-based currency unions, one in West Africa and the other in the South Pacific.
6. Again, past research has shown this to be true for nations in general. Again, see, Pollins (1989a and 1989b).
7. See e.g., Amsden (1987).
8. Again, please note that the values of South Korea's total trade are shown on the left side of figure 5.2. This is important because while the total trade curve is below and to the right of the per capita GDP curve, it is much larger in value as the different scales on the left and right y-axes make clear.
9. The strong relationship reported above between trade and GDP growth is similarly robust at one and three and one and four time lags as well. These models reveal that a $1 million increase in Korea's total trade led to an increase of just over $50 in its per capita GDP.

10. Like the previous figure, it is necessary to keep in mind the different scales of the two curves when examining the relationship between the two.

11. What is also important is that international trade became increasingly important in its contribution to Korea's GDP, growing from slightly over 15 percent of GDP in 1970 to just under 60 percent of GDP in 1995.

12. As a robustness check, we also used the total number of consulates and embassies in a country as our measure of diplomacy. The results of this analysis produced virtually identical results. We than a reviewer for this suggestion. At the same time all alternative tests and specifications are available upon request from the authors.

13. Data on South Korea's GDP and the trading partner country's GDP were obtained from World Development Indicators http://databank.worldbank.org/data/ (accessed 7/30/2014).

14. We will be able to test this proposition by comparing the results we obtain for the Cold War years with the post-Cold War, which we complete in the following chapter.

15. This measure is included in the model as the natural log of a nation's distance from South Korea.

16. We entered our two measures of a nation's political freedom and democracy into different models at a one-year lag.

17. The best examples of such nations would be China and the Soviet Union.

18. This population variable is entered into the models we estimate below at a one-year lag.

19. The value of "i" in equation is obtained because there are thirty-two years of observations on our over 180 dyads.

20. Wooldridge (2013), specifically, chapter 8.

21. We have provided these estimates along with other robustness tests, which are available from the authors upon request.

22. This estimation method can be problematic when sample sizes are smaller but given our large N associated with our data, we were confident in the results it produced.

23. Pollins (1989a and 1989b).

24. This would be Models 1 and 3, and the substantive impact of this variable was the same in both models.

Chapter Six

Diplomacy, Economic Development, and South Korea's Rise to International Influence

Our results for the Cold War and post-Cold War periods reinforce the idea that both international diplomatic and domestic economic factors worked together to help continue expanding South Korea's international trade levels and also to continue increasing its domestic economic prosperity. When we say they worked together, we are not saying that their impacts were parallel throughout both the Cold War and post-Cold War periods, because, as we have argued above, there was a temporal distinction in the way they worked, especially early in the post-Cold War years. Specifically, it was the increasing diplomatic successes of South Korea's leaders at a time when the country was still poor and far from being the prosperous and developed country it is today, that helped make possible the expansion of its international trade. This trade expansion then allowed for the increases that took place in South Korea's exports, which in turn helped spur the economic growth that increased as the end of the Cold War approached and continued into the post-1989 period.

The result was South Korea, early in the post-armistice period, being put on the path to becoming the influential middle power it is today. Again, what is important here is that this process began when South Korea was still a relatively poor nation, but what is also important is that this process has not only continued but also accelerated throughout the post-Cold War years. Indeed, South Korea's international rise continues to the present day as this once internationally isolated and poor nation continues to influence such important international organizations as the Development Assistance Committee of the OECD, not only adhering to the norms and practices of the world's most advanced nations but also utilizing its own experience as an erstwhile recipient of Official Development Assistance to guide the practices of donor nations so that their lending carries the maximum amount of economic benefit to recipient nations.

In light of these points, we have one remaining empirical analysis to complete, and this involves demonstrating that the factors we defined, calibrated, and analyzed above were also responsible for South Korea's rise to international influence. Specifically, we will need to determine just how well the diplomacy, economic growth and trade expansion, as well as other factors that we discussed and analyzed above, help explain the increases that occurred in South Korea's international status. This examination of the rise in South Korea's international influence will be conducted simultaneously for the Cold War years, during which time its rise began slowly but then accelerated, and the post-Cold War period, when South Korea's rise continued and resulted in it becoming the influential middle power it is today. This effort will begin with a discussion of how we plan to calibrate the international status of South Korea so that we can provide a statistical analysis of what factors contributed to this change in international importance that occurred throughout the post-Armistice period.

There is no singularly correct way to calibrate a nation's international status. Indeed, a number of possible option exist, and each is attendant to its own strengths and weaknesses. For our analysis of the factors that contributed to South Korea's rise to international influence, we utilize the measure developed as part of the Correlates of War Diplomatic Exchange Data project. While certainly not without its own weaknesses, which we will highlight below, this measure of a nation's "international status" not only serves our purposes better than other available measures, it also possesses strengths that we believe outweigh its potential weaknesses.[1] Moreover, the data that go into this measure are available for the entire time period that we are examining in this analysis, and the measure also contains observations for the one other country that we need to include in our analysis so as to ensure our assessment is complete.

There two parts to this measure, each of which captures an aspect of what goes into a nation's international status. The first refers specifically to how important a nation is diplomatically to other nations, something that is captured in the number of countries that establish and maintain formal diplomatic missions in its national capital. The logic behind this aspect of the measure rests on the notion that a number of characteristics of nations contribute to their being recognized by other nations as important and possessive of high international status. These characteristics can include economic capabilities that include the manufacture and export of highly desirable products and technology, and they can also include a nation's military prowess. In addition to these indicators, the number of diplomatic missions a nation has in its capital is also a characteristic indicative of it having a recognizably high international status. Indeed, establishing a formal diplomatic mission means that a nation decides to expend resources to maintain a diplomatic representative in a particular nation, say nation A, which in turn suggests that nation A is more important to the sending nation than another nation to which the sender does not expend resources to establish a formal diplomatic mission.

While the number of mission in a nation's capital is a strong indicator that sending nations consider it important enough to expend the resources necessary to have a presence there, there is still one more element to the international status indicator in the COW Diplomatic Exchange Data that concerns our measure. This second component allows us to evaluate just how one's nation's diplomatic importance compares to the diplomatic importance of all other nations. The indicator we employ accomplishes this by taking the number of missions a country has in its capital and then compares that number to the same number for the country that has the largest number of diplomatic missions in its national capital. When we say compare, we mean that the number of missions a nation has is then divided by the number of missions possessed by the country that is most sought after diplomatically. This makes the measure of international status we use a decimal indicating how close South Korea's diplomatic importance is to that of the most important nation. For the period of time under consideration in this analysis, this would be the United States, which had the largest number of formal diplomatic missions in Washington, DC.

With the variable to be explained defined, we turn next to the factors that account for the increases that occurred in South Korea's international status throughout the post-Armistice period. Two of the most important explanatory factors we discussed above are economic and refer, first, to the size of South Korea's Gross Domestic Product (GDP) and, second, the total amount of South Korean trade. In the analyses we conducted above, these two factors were closely related to each other and, as a result, we cannot include them in our models for estimation below at the same time. As a result, we include these factors separately in the two models we estimate below. We expect both of these economic factors to be positively related to South Korea's rise in international status, which will be indicated by our analysis producing statistically significant, substantively important, positive coefficients on each of these variables.

While we noted that the COW Diplomatic Exchange Data measure of international status had strengths that render it the best measure for the analysis we conduct below, but we also noted that it, like other measures, possesses some weaknesses. One of these concerns the fact that it is derivative of the diplomatic activities of South Korea and the nation to which its diplomatic successes are compared, the United States. For this reason, we cannot include a direct measure of South Korea's diplomatic successes in the models we estimate. This is not perfect for our analysis because we would like to include a measure of the number of diplomatic missions that South Korea had established throughout the period of time covered in our analysis. This is true because we would be interested in calibrating its direct impact on South Korea's international rise but also because it will allow us to test the impact of diplomatic reciprocity in our analysis. Nonetheless, this issue does not undermine our efforts to explain what accounts for South Korea' international rise for two reasons.

The first is simply that South Korea's diplomatic successes are embedded in our measure of international status because of South Korea's diplomatic successes being part of the manner in which that measure is constructed. The second reason is that we can include an important diplomatic factor in the analysis we conduct below, and this refers back to the international competition that South Korea faced with respect to the international efforts of leaders in Pyongyang. While this competition for international legitimacy and support was particularly acute when the peninsular version of the Hallstein Doctrine was in operation, both North and South Korea still competed for international recognition and favor even after this restriction was abandoned and both nations maintained formal diplomatic relations with the same country. We capture this diplomatic competition between Seoul and Pyongyang in our analysis by including the international status of North Korea in our models. This indicator is measured the same way we calibrated South Korea's international status.

Next, we turn to the impact of history in our analysis of what factors account for the increases in international status that South Korea experienced throughout the post-armistice period. First, we must capture the impact that the international system had on South Korea prior to the tearing down of the Berlin Wall. This is important for the overall argument we have made in the preceding chapters that it was during the Cold War, when South Korea was still a poor country, that its leaders took action to remove it from the international isolation it experienced after the Korean War and reconnect it with all available nations. South Korea's leaders faced constraints during these years, not simply because it was still poor and did not have the economic resources it currently has, but also because international relations during the Cold War were hierarchical and more rigid than when the Berlin Wall collapsed. Nonetheless, it is during the Cold War period that South Korea's leaders put the country on the path to the elevated international status it has today, and to capture this impact we include the Cold War period as a dummy variable.

In addition to this, we know that the ending of the Cold War in Europe was a watershed event in international affairs that led to more diplomatic opportunities for South Korea's leaders. This is because nations that were either not available because of alliance attachments or unwilling because of sympathies resting with the communist nations of the world would now consider having formal diplomatic relations with Seoul. As a result, we must capture the impact of these international changes in our analysis, which we accomplish by including three additional variables. These variables refer to three presidential administrations, specifically, that of Kim Young-Sam, Kim Dae-Jung, and Roh Moo-Hyun.

Kim Young-Sam had an important presidential administration because he was the first civilian elected to the South Korean presidency since the country transitioned to democratic politics. The next two presidential administrations, the Kim Dae-Jung and the Roh Moo-Hyun Administrations, are significant because they were presidents who were freely elected by South Korea's citizens, but more importantly because they represented the first freely elected progressive administrations in South Korea. As mentioned above, these two administrations carried out what is known as the Sunshine Policy toward North Korea whereby South Korea engaged in unconditional interactions with Pyongyang as an act of good faith. Including these two regimes as dummy variables will allow us to capture any diplomatic differences attendant to administrations that more freely engaged with Pyongyang without the quid pro quo approach of their predecessors.

Finally, we include two more variables in our analysis. The first of these is a control variable to distinguish South Korea's level of democracy, which will capture the growing level of influences exerted by the South Korean voting public in the foreign policy decisions of its leaders. Next, we need to include factors that capture the fact that the data we use for this analysis are time series data, which means that we have to pay attention to issues that are part of using data where values at one point in time are important for values on our dependent variable later in time. This requires that we first be certain to model time in an appropriate way in the models we estimate below. We capture these effects by the inclusion of a simple time trend which we include in our models, which we expect to have a positive impact on South Korea's status. Moreover, as part of our time series analysis, we include variables that capture the impact of the fact that we estimate autoregressive, moving average models to get reliable estimates of the impacts of the factors we have noted will have an impact on the international status of South Korea from 1960 to 2015.

With our dependent variable defined and those factors that will determine South Korea's international status specified, we note that the model for specification is as follows:

$$Y_t = \mathrm{a} + \beta_1 X_i^1 + \ldots + \beta_K X_t^K + \mathrm{e}_i \quad \mathrm{i} = 3{,}383 \ \mathrm{i} = 56, \qquad (2)$$

where Y_{it} is a continuously valued, unobserved variable estimating South Korea's international status in a year for the period under consideration, and $X_i^{1.K}$ is a one by nine vector containing the covariates. From the above discussion, recall that two the covariates are continuous measures, the first is a measure of South Korea's Gross Domestic Product in a year for the period under consideration, and the second is a measure that captures the total amount of international trade engaged in by South Korea in a year for the period under consideration. Four of the covariates are dummy variables that capture the effect of the Cold War period, the impact of the Kim Yong-Sam Administration, and the impact of the next two progressive administrations, those of Kim Dae-Jung and Roh Moo-Hyun. Two of the three remaining covariates are discrete variables, one of which is a time trend and the other captures the level of democracy in South Korea. The final variable is a ratio which is a measure of international competition from North Korea, captured by North Korea's international status, which is measured in the same way as South Korea's international status is measured in the COW Diplomatic Exchange Data.

The results of conducting this analysis of what helps account for South Korea's growing international status are presented in table 6.1. We see from the data in the table that the estimation of two AR(1) models, one using trade as an independent variable and the other using South Korea's GDP produced reliable results, which we see from the significance of statistics on our AR(1) processes and the Sigma statistics for those of our moving averages. Also, the results indicated that our expectations are generally confirmed about what explains South Korea's rising international status but not without some results that we did not anticipate. First, we see that the coefficients on our time trend were statistically insignificant in both models with signs in different directions in each model. While we expected time to be negative and significant, this result is best explained by the fact that our models contained other factors that captured the impacts associated with different sub-periods in the years covered by our analysis.

Most important was the statistically significant, positive coefficient on the dummy variable for the period of the Cold War. This is an important result that confirms the overall argument of this volume that South Korea was well on its way to international influence before the end of the Cold War when rapid economic growth made it the prosperous nation it is today. Indeed, it was during the Cold War that South Korea's leaders removed it from the international isolation it was in after the Korean War and reconnected it numerous nations, even with the constraints they faced in a Cold War international system. These results are strengthened with the coefficients on the three post-Cold War presidential administrations, which we included as factors to capture the new opportunities and challenges South Korean leaders

Table 6.1. Explaining the Rise in South Korea's International Status, 1960–2015

	Model 1 (GDP)	*Model 2 (Trade)*
Time	–0.405	0.309
	(0.553)	(0.349)
$ln\text{GDP}_{t-1}$	18.67**	—
	(6.539)	
$ln\text{Trade}_{t-1}$	—	5.479*
		(2.327)
Level of Democracy$_{t-1}$	–0.317***	–0.328***
	(0.0859)	(0.0791)
North Korea's Rank$_{t-1}$	0.470*	0.439+
	(0.238)	(0.232)
Cold War	5.544***	5.152***
	(1.041)	(0.704)
Kim Young-Sam Administration	–4.251*	–4.119*
	(1.687)	(1.817)
Kim Dae-Jung Administration	–5.175*	–4.942*
	(2.190)	(2.235)
Roh Moo-Hyun Administration	–4.800*	–4.519*
	(2.086)	(2.051)
Constant	–174.8**	–36.16*
	(59.62)	(14.27)
ARMA		
AR (1)	0.938***	0.965***
	(0.0649)	(0.0257)
Sigma (ϱ)	1.633***	1.669***
	(0.148)	(0.142)
No. of obs.	56	56
Durbin-Watson *d* statistic	1.8119	1.6440
AIC	237.9921	241.0067
BIC	260.271	263.2856

Note: Dependent variables are the proportion of the number of Korea's embassies established and maintained abroad to the total number of US's embassies established and maintained abroad. Semirobust standard errors in parentheses.

Significance Level: + $p<0.10$, * $p<0.05$, ** $p<0.01$, *** $p<0.001$.

faced in the years after the Berlin Wall came down. Results for the two Kim administrations and the Roh Moo-Hyun administration all indicate that South Korea's rise in international status was much slower during their tenures than at any time in the years of the Cold War. This does not mean that there was no progress during these post-Cold War years but rather that it was the Cold War period, more than any other time in the post-armistice period, when the road to South Korea's international influence was paved.

One unexpected result rested with our estimated impact of diplomatic competition from North Korea on the efforts of South Korea's leaders to raise their country's international status, which we expected to be statistically significant and negative. The results in table 6.1, however, tell us that, in both the trade and GDP models, North Korea's rise in international status positively affected that of South Korea, albeit in a substantively small manner. Moreover, the impact of North Korea's international status was not statistically significant in the trade model. Contrary to these results, the impacts associated with our two economic factors, South Korea's gross domestic product (GDP) and its total international trade, were statistically significant with signs in the expected direction. Moreover, the substantive impact was much greater in the case of South Korea's GDP than it was for international trade. This was expected because we know that the increasing size of South Korea's GDP increasingly made available economic wherewithal that South Korea then employed to pursue desired foreign policy goals. Moreover, while the results indicate that trade did have a smaller independent impact on South Korea's rise to international influence, results provided in the previous chapter revealed that it was diplomacy that helped increase levels of South Korea's international trade.

NOTES

1. See e.g., Ward (2017) for a criticism of the measure we utilize and a discussion of some alternative measures. Among his criticisms are problems with the manner in which some factors reveal inconsistencies in the way they should correlate with other aspects of the measure. We do not deny the existence of the inconsistencies that Ward (2017) has revealed, but we do note that these criticisms are based on judgements of leaders' diplomatic preferences and, thus, more normative than positive. As a result, they are not that applicable to the analysis we conduct below.

Chapter Seven

The Present and Future of South Korea's International Influence

Showing the pivotal role that diplomacy played in South Korea's rise to international influence is an important contribution that the analyses presented above have provided. Indeed, that it was the diplomatic successes of leaders early in the post-armistice period that led directly to the expansion of South Korean trade and was not only an essential part of its domestic economic development strategy but also what helped place South Korea on the path to its international rise as an important middle power has either been missed or understated in the scholarly literature. Moreover, that it was not rapid economic growth alone but that both diplomatic and economic factors continually contributed to South Korea's international rise in both the Cold War and post-Cold War periods is also an important contribution of the analyses and discussions we have provided thus far. In spite of this, what renders a theoretically informed statistical analysis and the results it produces a significant scholarly contribution is not simply that it offers a more comprehensive explanation for a phenomenon like South Korea's rise to international influence but, more importantly, whether or not it can provide additional purchase on related phenomena that are yet to unfold completely.

Our specific reference here is to the fact that South Korea currently faces a number of security challenges in the East Asia region,[1] and these challenges have been developing over the last two decades and have generated a number of debates among South Korean leaders about its role as a regionally important actor and what strategic policy choices it needs to make to deal with evolving challenges. Moreover, given that South Korea's rise to international influence has also rendered it one of the world's increasingly significant middle powers, we must also explore what the analysis we provided above suggests for how it will continue in this important international role. A scholarly analysis that offers insight into how South Korea is likely to respond to the regional and international challenges it faces and what impact its response will have on interstate relations, both regionally and globally, will have a broader and, thus, more valuable scholarly impact. In the sections that follow, we explore how the explanation for South Korea's international rise we offered herein helps us address these important questions.

The challenges South Korea faces in the East Asian region and the policy debate these challenges have engendered are so very important because of how South Korea responds will touch directly not only on the post-armistice alliance structure that has provided an environment of peace and stability in the region but also on its overall international status.[2] This is because it was the environment of peace and stability that the East Asian Alliance helped provide that supported the economic development and international rise of South Korea and other nations in the region. In spite of its overall positive impact since the end of the Korean War, this alliance structure, defined by triangular relations between the United States and South Korea and Japan, is under more strain now than at any time in the past.[3] Given that the end of this alliance structure is one possible result of how South Korea responds to the region's challenges, and given that we do not know how such a development would impact stability in the region and, thus, the environment that supported South Korea's international rise, we need a perspective to help us understand not simply what South Korea has done to meet the challenges it has faced thus far but one that can offer a way to determine how it will behave in the future and what this will mean for the international relations in the East Asian region and around the globe.

In light of the challenges facing South Korea, we will investigate how it is likely to contend with the region's changing power dynamics as they unfold by calibrating how both its continually successful diplomatic efforts and domestic growth and increasing economic wherewithal—factors that led to its rise to international influence—will shape the policy debate that has been occurring among its leaders over the most appropriate action to meet the challenges it faces and continue to elevate itself as an influential middle power. We begin this effort by laying out the assumptions that form the basis of our assessment.

The results we discussed in the previous chapters revealed that South Korea used the tools of diplomacy and its increasing economic wherewithal in both the Cold War and post-Cold War periods to expand its international trade, grow its domestic economy, raise the prosperity levels of its people, and continue to elevate its international status so that it could become the influential middle power it is today. Given what these two sets of factors allowed this nation to achieve, we proceed from the assumption that is leaders have no incentive to abandon employing a mix of these two factors to protect and expand its trading relationships and status as it faces the region's evolving security challenges. Moreover, given that it was the peace and stability of the East Asian region that was provided by the East Asian alliance that offered the supportive environment for South Korea to achieve its domestic and international goals, we also assume that South Korea's leaders would use both their diplomatic and economic assets to maintain the robustness of this alliance system.

To know if the challenges that South Korean leaders face in the East Asian region can be managed by its leaders employing the tools of diplomacy and economic statecraft in a way that maintains the integrity and effectiveness of the East Asian alliance structure that supported its growth and international elevation, we must first provide a discussion of the specific challenges that South Korea faces. The first of these involves an increasingly powerful and assertive China, which has led to an evolution in the region's power dynamics. This challenge of a rising China begins with the fact that the People's Republic of China (PRC) has become the world's second largest economy, overtaking Japan for this position in 2010. It was able to accomplish this milestone because its economy sustained very high levels of growth for more than three decades. This development has naturally made more economic resources available to the PRC's leaders to achieve their international goals, which in and of itself has changed the international dynamics of the East Asian region.

In addition to its economic rise, China has, at the same time, substantially increased its military strength, and this includes vast improvements in its military hardware. Specifically, in the last two to three decades, China has accumulated several thousand aircraft, and it is currently in the process of producing its next generation of fighter aircraft, which its military leaders intended to be able to challenge the United States's new generation F-35 fighter. It has also accumulated an extensive array of artillery and other sources of firepower to support its land forces of well over 2 million soldiers. Finally, it has built a blue-water navy that consists of nearly two hundred vessels of different sizes and types, including an aircraft carrier that will in a short time be joined by another.

The size of the Chinese economy, the growing power of its military, and its increasing assertiveness in the region are facts that many democratic nations recognize as a challenge to peace and stability in East Asia and potentially throughout the world. What makes these empirical facts more troubling and, thus, constituting a challenge that has encouraged South Korean leaders to think about a possible alternative path to ensure continuation of its post-armistice achievements is the question of what China plans to do in the region with its growing might. China has increasingly asserted itself in the region to advance its interests. Indeed, as one analyst has noted, "China persistently makes every effort to expand its influence over neighboring countries that it believes are under Beijing's strategic scope."[4] While the scope of China's strategic interests are currently more focused on the nations that rim the East and South China Seas, its growing economic and military power has directly affected interstate relations in Northeast Asia and elsewhere.

As stated briefly above, China's economic and military rise has led to changing power dynamics in the East Asia region that has directly affected South Korea's relations with the United States and Japan as well as how Seoul manages its interactions with Pyongyang. These impacts are important in and of themselves, but China's rise and growing assertiveness in the region is even more of a concern to South Korean leaders for one other reason. The reference here is to whether a rising China that continually extends its influence in the region and around the globe will be a revisionist power or one that conforms to current international norms, strengthening the institutions and processes that form the current liberal international order. This is important for South Korea because it is under the postwar liberal international order that it was able to become the increasingly influential middle power it is today.

If China is peaceful in its rise, it will in a general way adhere to the current array of international norms that govern interstate relations and, thus, be more likely to seek and achieve accommodation with the United States and other Western and Asian powers on issues of contention. If this accurately describes the manner in which China's growing economic and military presence will occur, South Korea will not have to consider abandoning its alliance with the United States but will then implement minor changes in the way that it promotes peace and security in the region to accommodate the region's changing power dynamics.

On the other hand, if China is truly a revisionist power bent on remaking the norms and institutions that govern interstate relations in the region, and around the globe, South Korea will be put under increasing pressure to accommodate Chinese demands. This means closing the distance that exists between Seoul and Beijing while, at the same time, putting more distance between itself and the United States and Japan. This scenario can put the East Asian alliance under more strain, but it does not necessarily spell an end to its alliance with the United States nor its accommodation efforts with respect to Tokyo. Nonetheless, it does mean that South Korea's place in the East Asian alliance may undergo modifications as an increasingly powerful China asserts its demands in the region.

South Korean leaders have been discussing a number of possible changes in its foreign policy as a potential response to the growing influence of China, and the choices available to leaders have been aptly summarized in Snyder

(2018). Snyder's discussion of South Korea's options is informed by a framework where leaders select from a range of choices on two interacting continua where one relates to the U.S.-South Korean alliance and whether to maintain it or abandon it and the other concerns South Korea's overall foreign policy approach that is bounded at the extremes by an inwardly oriented, parochial point of view or an outwardly oriented, international approach. This general framework leads to several distinct choice possibilities for South Korea's leaders that can include doing nothing to engaging in a major revision of its overall foreign policy approach as well as moving significantly in the direction of accommodating China or maintaining its distance while keeping its relations with Washington and Tokyo close and robust. While Snyder's discussion is informative and insightful, the options he lays out for South Korea refer more to end states rather than specific policy initiatives that can be employed to address the challenge of a rising China to maintain the peace and security Seoul has enjoyed in the post-armistice period.

The point is that what specific policy initiatives South Korean leaders will engage in will clearly be conditioned by how China's rise affects the region's power dynamics and how these changing dynamics will affect South Korea' primary foreign goal of maintaining those features of Asian interstate relations as well as the liberal postwar international order, both of which facilitated South Korea's rise to international influence. This is because it was a stable security environment in Northeast Asia and well as a larger set of international norms and institutions that provided a supportive context within which post-armistice leaders in Seoul could achieve the domestic economic and international diplomacy goals that allowed it to achieve the rise to international influence that it achieved. As discussed above, China's rise is the principal challenge to maintaining these supportive contexts, both regionally and globally, but there are two other challenges that South Korea faces that will also have an impact on its foreign policy decision making.

The second challenge facing South Korean leaders relates to an increasingly provocative North Korea that has crossed the nuclear threshold. Provocations from North Korea are nothing new, and there have been times when North Korea has engaged in provocative behavior that has been outright belligerent. For example, in September 1983, North Korean agents attempted to assassinate then South Korean president, Chun Doo-Hwan and members of his cabinet in Rangoon, Burma.[5] While President Chun escaped this assassination attempt, seventeen South Korean officials, including the deputy prime minister and two cabinet members were killed. This was a very violent event that reduced the credibility of the regime in Pyongyang, and, fortunately, when the event passed, it was followed by more than a decade of relative quiescence. Tensions again increased at the end of the 1990s when there was a naval clash near Yeonpyeong Island. This was followed three years later by another naval engagement and then again in 2009 and 2010. In the engagement of 2010, a South Korean naval vessel, the corvette *Cheonon*, was sunk leaving a number of crew members missing.[6]

While dangerous engagements such as these occurred at different points throughout these years, North Korea's nuclear development program was a constant, and it reached many notable milestones, particularly in the last five years. By the end of 2017, North Korea had conducted several successful nuclear tests. These tests were underground explosions of thermonuclear weapons, and reports based on seismic data led to varying estimates of the kilotonage of these explosions, some as high as 120 kilotons. At the same time, North Korea has continued the testing of its delivery systems for the nuclear warheads it has been developing, which has also resulted in a number of breakthroughs. North Korea's first missile tests go back to the early 1990s when it successfully fired a Nodong-1 missile into the Sea of Japan.[7] These test have continued intermittently since then and, in the last few years, have revealed some notable successes. A 2014 test of the existing Nodong-1 missile was of a more advanced design. This test was followed by successful tests beginning in the spring and summer of 2017 and continuing until the late spring of 2018 of more advanced missiles. These missile tests revealed that Pyongyang had completed a successful test of an intercontinental ballistic missile, the Hwasong 12 that was followed later by a successful launch of the Hwasong 14. Analysts calculated that these delivery systems were capable of reaching the United States.

Naturally, South Korean leaders are ever focused on the behavior of the regime in Pyongyang, and North Korea's provocations lead South Korea to conclude that a continuation of the alliance with the United States was not only useful but necessary as a deterrent. Moreover, given that North Korean provocations, particularly its most recent missile tests, also threaten Japan and the United States, South Korea has an incentive to maintain the alliance in order to be a moderating influence. Consequently, North Korean provocations are very unlikely to encourage leaders in Seoul to consider any substantive change in its military relationship with the United States. However, there is another part to South Korea's relationship with the United States that may encourage leaders to think about the alliance and South Korea's role in countering threats from the North and promoting its security interests in the region. The reference here is to the differing levels of engagement from South Korea's principal ally in the region, the United States.

When we use the phrase differing levels of engagement, we do not mean that the United States has threatened to abandon South Korea by abrogating its alliance commitment with Seoul but rather that its actual level of engagement in the political, economic, and security affairs of this region has waxed and waned depending on how pressing other commitments were for the United States.[8] Since the terrorist attacks of 9/11, the United States has spent a large amount of time focused on the war on terrorism. This was particularly true for the presidential administration of George W. Bush, and it continued into the early years of the Obama Administration until he initiated a major change in the United States's foreign policy orientation, known as the pivot to Asia. In 2011, the Obama Administration announced that American foreign policy would become more focused on the Asia-Pacific Region in an effort to mitigate the destabilizing influence of both North Korea and China in an effort to help U.S. allies counter the rising economic and military power of China.[9] This reorientation of U.S. foreign policy was welcomed by U.S. allies because U.S. commitments in the Middle East, Afghanistan, and elsewhere outside of Asian rendered its leadership level in the Asia-Pacific region less than what was necessary to deal adequately with the challenges that it and its allies face there.[10]

The Trump Administration shared its predecessor's concerns with China and North Korea, albeit its rhetoric was initially more negative toward the former and potentially more threatening toward the latter. Parallel with its approach to North Korea and China, the Trump Administration also called for its Japanese and South Korean allies—and its allies in Europe and elsewhere for that matter—to increase their share of their respective regions' defense burdens, and this represented a substantive departure from the orientation of previous administrations' approach to the United States's relations with its allies in East Asia and elsewhere. This is important because it has rendered U.S. efforts in the region more challenging than they already are, and this is true despite the periodic toning down of rhetoric toward China and North Korea. Nonetheless, there is evidence that the initial rise in regional tension may be abated in the medium term because of the Singapore summit with North Korea, the fact that another summit has been scheduled, and the fact that the United States in engaged in ongoing trade negotiations with China, avoiding a threatened rise in tariffs.

There are two reasons the United States's varying levels of engagement, especially under the current Trump Administration, will render South Korea's efforts to preserve the Northeast Asian alliance system and work to maintain the global context that supported its growth and its increasing international status more challenging. The first is the Trump Administration's "America First" emphasis, which has elevated the importance of narrowly defined economic issues, making it difficult to maintain the longstanding separation that has existed between peace and security concerns and issues surrounding trade and economics.[11] This elevated stress on economic issues and the calling out of countries—even allies—because of claims that they have taken advantage of the United States, can serve as a distraction, keeping the United States and South Korea from remaining focused on the greatest threat to the status quo in the region, the economic and military rise of China.

The second reason that the United States's varying levels of engagement in the region will render the task of South Korea preserving the status quo more difficult is the response of the Trump Administration to North Korea's testing of increasingly advanced missiles. Perhaps the best way to characterize the current administration's response to Pyongyang possessing a missile that can potentially reach U.S. cities has not been to work more closely with U.S. allies in Tokyo and Seoul, which any reasoned response will need to include. Rather, the Trump Administration, at least initially, led an effort in the United Nations to ratchet up economic pressure on the North while criticizing Beijing for not doing enough to halt North Korea's weapons development program. This initial approach elicited equally bellicose responses from Pyongyang and led to an increasingly hyperbolic rhetoric that only increased the fear and suspicion of leaders in Pyongyang over U.S. intentions. Fortunately, the Trump Administration subsequently toned down its rhetoric and used its celebrity to schedule a summit whereby, for the first time since the DPRK was established, the leaders of the United States and North Korea met and discussed the issues that separated the two countries.

Despite a notable reduction in tensions between the Pyongyang and Seoul and North Korea and the United States, the issues that make North Korea a problem for interstate relations in Northeast Asia remain unresolved. This means that there are serious challenges that South Korean leaders face with respect to its primary ally in the region, and they complicate efforts of Seoul and its allies to preserve the peace and security the region has generally witnessed since the end of the Korean War. In light of these challenges, we have two expectations with respect to Seoul's strategy going forward, and, to understand this strategy, we must first keep in mind that the context of interstate relations in East Asia is defined by triangular relations among the United States, South Korea, and Japan where the United States has separate alliances with both Seoul and Tokyo.[12]

Despite various levels of U.S. engagement and tensions between Seoul and Tokyo, it is this alliance structure that has helped preserve South Korea's security and, thus, provided a context that supported its diplomatic successes and domestic economic growth that combined to lead to its rise to international influence and being the important middle power it is today. As a result, our first expectation is that South Korea will prefer to keep this alliance structure intact while agreeing to adjustments at the margins as changing conditions in the region will require. Second, we also expect that South

Korea will employ all of the diplomatic skills and economic resources it can to accomplish this goal.

In terms of specific actions, we expect leaders in South Korea to follow an approach where minor adjustments, defined as making overtures to satisfy Chinese demands will be made by South Korea's leaders, and these will involve economic and political initiatives. Specifically, we will expect that South Korea will continue to increase its trading relations with China and also support a growth in business relations between Chinese and South Korean companies. We also expect that South Korean policy toward China will involve certain political overtures that give the appearance of Seoul moving closer to Beijing. However, these political overtures will be limited and not cross a threshold that indicates South Korea abandoning its alliance with the United States nor forgoing efforts to maintain healthy relations with Japan.

By making these kinds of adjustments, South Korea can buy time and reduce pressure from China, but, at the same time, it can also maintain its alliance with the United States and Japan and preserve the conditions that allowed its international rise to occur. To this end, South Korean leaders will use the tools it has employed in the past to serve its interests in the region and around the globe, meeting the challenges of the changing economic and power dynamics that define interstate relations in East Asia and throughout the world. These include employing the substantial economic resources that its rapid economic development and consequent GDP expansion have provided and relying on the advanced diplomatic skills its leaders have evolved over the years of its international successes throughout the post-armistice period. South Korean leaders will use these tools to build support for its efforts to contain the provocative behavior of its adversary in the North, to appease the increasing demands of China—short of moving fully into its orbit—and also doing what is necessary to keep its principal ally engaged in the region, maintaining the security system as well as the international institutions and norms that have provided the supportive environment it enjoyed throughout the post armistice period.

THE CONTINUITY OF THE PAST

The challenges that South Korea faces both regionally and globally have been developing for some time, and we can use its policy responses thus far to serve as a guide for how we expect it will continue to grapple with such challenges well into the future. Concerning North Korea, we see evidence that our assessment of Seoul's expected behavior, even in the face of Pyongyang crossing a new nuclear threshold, is supported. This is true because the current administration of Moon Jae-In is in South Korea's progressive tradition, which means it is more concerned with engaging with the North than recording identifiable concessions from Pyongyang. As a result, leaders in Seoul have continued to use their economic and diplomatic resources to engage the North in an effort to reduce tensions on the peninsula, and this includes supporting the Trump Administration's efforts to meet with the North Korean leader more than once.

There is little doubt that the South Korean leadership, as well as leaders in the United States and around the globe, all would have preferred that North Korea would have kept its weapons program short of the threshold it has crossed. This is because the path that led Pyongyang to this point has been defined by ongoing provocations and overall unpredictable outbursts. The North's recent turn to a less provocative, if not more cooperative, approach to the United States and Seoul has resulted in a significant reduction in tensions on the Korean Peninsula and a more stable set of inter-Korean relations. This has led current leaders in South Korea continue their engagement approach with Pyongyang, using Seoul's economic tools and diplomatic skills to engage with the North when such behavior promised a reduction in tensions.

There are a number of illustrations of how South Korea has approached the North by using a combination of economic and diplomatic engagement tools in the context of an overall deterrence strategy. This is not to say that every leader elected to the South Korean presidency will behave in exactly the same way toward the North, because they are distinguished by their employment of quid pro quo tactics in their approach to Pyongyang. Specifically, the previous two presidencies of Lee Myung-Bak and Park Geun-Hye were more reluctant to engage in certain overtures without positive responses from North Korea, but the current regime of President Moon Jae-In, which is in the vein of the previous administrations of Kim Dae-Jung and Roh Moo-Hyun, has been more willing to engage the North without prior evidence of a positive response. This engagement approach of the current Moon Administration has been encouraged by the holding of a summit between the president of the United States and North Korean leader, Kim Jong-Un. While the goal of coming to an agreement on a way to eliminate all of the North's nuclear weapons was not attained, cooperation between Seoul and Pyongyang has continued. Moreover, the scheduling of a follow up summit will most likely continue and relations between North and South Korea will remain relatively quiescent and stable.[13]

The current state of lowered tension in inter-Korean relations—tensions that were initially increased by the hyperbolic rhetoric of the Trump Administration toward North Korean leader, Kim Jung-Un—aptly characterize how the South Korean strategy of employing its diplomatic resources and tools of economic statecraft can result in outcomes that are desired by leaders in Seoul. While North Korea has not abandoned its nuclear capabilities, its provocative testing of missile technology has temporarily ceased and rhetoric between Seoul and Pyongyang is much less disruptive. Perhaps the most notable illustration of how South Korea's use of diplomacy and economic incentives has led to positive results concerns how meetings held in the demilitarized zone led to an agreement that a delegation from Pyongyang would be able to compete in the 2018 Winter Olympics in Pyeongchang. In fact, South Korean leaders went so far as to not simply allow numerous North Korean athletes to compete in five Olympic sports but they also agreed to the two countries marching together in the opening and closing ceremonies and to putting together a unified, North-South female ice hockey team.[14]

This was a significant development that has clearly helped ameliorate what had become a very tense environment, especially in light of the vitriolic exchanges that initially occurred between Kim Jong-Un and President Donald Trump. Moreover, this is a very welcome development in the region, but it did not come about without South Korea providing significant concessions to the North. These include Seoul agreeing to cease urging defections from the North and, perhaps most importantly, not pressing the North on its weapons program.[15] In fact, although it did cease its provocative testing of missiles, the North did not make any real concessions on its nuclear weapons program. This is clearly undesirable but nonetheless acceptable to the Moon Administration, which had pledged to be more engaging with the North so that it could reduce tensions on the Peninsula, which it set as a principal goal in inter-Korean relations. While negotiating an agreement for the North's participation in the 2018 Winter Games may have been approached differently by previous administrations without some willingness on the part of Pyongyang to compromise on its weapons programs, the point is that this affair is illustrative of South Korean leaders employing their diplomatic and economic resources to keep relations with North Korea as stable as possible until a more permanent solution can be reached.

Up to now, South Korea has also shown willingness to use its diplomatic and economic resources to maintain its relationship with the United States, particularly, the alliance structure that is based on triangular relations with the United States and Japan. This goal faced an immediate challenge when Donald Trump took office because of his administration's "America-First" strategy, which put pressure on U.S. allies to contribute more to providing for their own defense and to be open to renegotiating existing trade deals. With respect to Seoul, the Trump Administration directed the United States Trade Representative (USTR) to inform South Korean leaders that the United States would pull out completely of the U.S.-South Korean Free Trade agreement unless Seoul showed willingness to accept certain amendments. Because South Korean leaders agreed to make changes to the original Free Trade Agreement with the United States (KORUS FTA), the Trump Administration agreed in return to exempt South Korea from the 25 percent tariff it had imposed on global steel. This required South Korea to adhere to a strict quota on the amount of steel it exported to the U.S.

In addition to its willingness to amend the Korea-U.S. Free Trade Agreement, there are other instances of South Korean leaders taking accommodating positions toward the United States. Two of these are of particular note because they aptly illustrate just how far Seoul is willing to go to maintain good relations with the United States. In these examples, South Korea's leaders, like leaders in other nations allied with the United States, recognized that more efforts will have to be made to accede to demands made by the new Trump Administration. President Moon Jae-In did something in this spirit that had not been done since the Administration of Ronald Reagan. While all U.S. presidents have made visits to Seoul as part of their Asian tours, President Reagan was unique in that he made his visit to South Korea an official state visit. Such visits are much more involved affairs that begin with an official invitation from the South Korean president, and that is what President Moon did for the Trump Administration. By making President Trump's visit to South Korea official, it put the relationship with this administration on a better footing than when the administration first took office.

A second example of accommodating action taken by leaders in South Korea refers back to the Korea-U.S. Free Trade Agreement discussed above. This agreement, KORUS FTA was very long in the making, encountered numerous difficulties, and ultimately required some very undesirable compromises on the part of both sides to be brought to fruition. Nonetheless, in the fall of 2017, the Moon Administration agreed to begin talks that would address the concerns of the current U.S. president. These negotiations were completed in the late summer of 2018, and it is difficult to understate the extent to which this represents a concession on the part of South Korea to accommodate its main ally. Consider that, during the 2016 presidential campaign and shortly after the inauguration of Donald Trump, officials in the South Korean Ministry of Foreign Affairs and Trade (MOFAT) issued statements that there would be no renegotiation of this agreement whatsoever. Consequently, the fact that there was a renegotiated free trade agreement with the United States represents a significant South Korean concession.

We can see similar efforts on the part of the South Korean leadership with respect to accommodating the increasing demands of China, although Seoul's accommodating actions toward Beijing have not gone as far as they have with respect to the United States. In 2016, relations between Seoul and Beijing had soured when President Park Geun-Hye agreed to host the Terminal High Altitude Area Defense (THAAD) system that was developed by the United States. Chinese leaders saw this move by South Korea as a threat to the country's essential interests in the region, and expressed a strong disapproval to the government in Seoul. Chinese officials even engaged in unofficial economic sanctions against Seoul since 2016. This tense situation lasted for just over a year as President Moon Jae-In agreed that no more anti-ballistic missile systems would be placed in South Korea.[16]

Before this accord could be reached, South Korea engaged in a number of initiatives that were designed to placate Beijing, and these included increasing the number of economic, cultural, and educational exchanges that occurred between the two countries. Seoul even agreed to join the Asian Infrastructure and Investment Bank (AIIM), which the United States strongly opposed because it was a Chinese effort to undermine such U.S.-backed financial institutions as the World Bank and Asian Development Bank. This does not mean that South Korea's efforts vis-à-vis Beijing were strictly the result of the THAAD problem because Seoul had also engaged in accommodating behavior before President Park Geun-Hye agreed to host the THAAD radar system. To that end, in September 2015, President Park visited Beijing and observed a military parade from a place near Tiananmen Gate reserved for Chinese friends. This was President Park's sixth summit with the Chinese and her sixth visit to Beijing.

Current South Korean president Moon Jae-In also visited China and has more visits scheduled. Prior to his first visit in early 2018, President Moon made certain overtures to reduce tensions and forge agreements that would put Sino-South Korean relations on a less tense path. Most importantly, President Moon agreed that he would work with Chinese leader, Xi Jin-Ping to increase economic, cultural, and education exchanges between the two countries. As stated above, President Moon also made the commitment that South Korea would not allow the U.S. to engage in ballistic missile deployments on the Peninsula and that South Korea would not participate in any U.S. sponsored ballistic missile defense effort. China, on the other hand, would seek closer diplomatic ties with Seoul and would also end its unofficial imposition of economic sanctions.

These efforts on the part of the South Korea have clearly been designed to placate Beijing, suggesting that Seoul is moving into a continuously closer relationship with the People's Republic of China. In addition to this, South Korea's leaders are most likely to continue to use their diplomatic and economic resources to appease the evolving demands of Beijing. Even though this accommodating behavior is viewed with concern by some observers in Washington, DC, and even in Tokyo, it is not likely to lead to any disruption in the U.S.-South Korea alliance. Chung and Kim (2016) noted that South Korea will not trust China even though it has become more involved with it in terms of economic, cultural and educational exchanges. South Korea will continue to be engaged with the United States in order to placate the United States and keep inter-Korean relations on the recently established quiescent path they are following. This is especially true as long as Beijing continues to treat North Korea in a manner that swings between support and distance but does not exert any real pressure to alter its weapons policies. Moreover, Kim and Cha (2016) have noted that this appears to be the best approach not just because it will be the best strategy to preserve the environment that supported its economic growth and rise to international influence, but it is an approach that is most likely to result in positive-sum benefits.

Overall, what these events and developments indicate is that, in spite of the real challenges that South Korea faces in maintaining a peaceful and supportive environment in the region and, thus, continuing its role as an influential middle power, the incentives that have encouraged South Korea's leaders to put their country on the path to prosperity and international influence will be those who also help them keep their country on the path it has been on for many decades. This will mean continuing to use the economic and diplomatic tools at their disposal to reduce tensions with the North while maintaining a strong deterrent against attack, engaging in accommodating behavior with China, and doing what is necessary to maintain its military alliance with the United States.

This does not mean that South Korea's leaders will avoid any action that may be opposed by one of more of these countries because this is likely to oc cur from time to time. It also does not mean that there can be no change in the region's interstate relations that would alter the incentives that have encouraged continuity in the South Korea's current approach. There are changes that could occur in the region's power dynamics or in the international system overall that might lead South Korea to cease maintaining its alliance with the United States and moving more clearly into the Chinese orbit. However, short of another outright war with North Korea or a complete withdrawal of the United States from the Korean Peninsula, the incentives that have governed South Korean strategy in the past are likely to persist.

NOTES

1. We are referring to three challenges in particular: the rise of China, the growing unpredictability of a North Korea that has crossed the nuclear threshold, and a United States that has at times wavered in its commitment to the region.

2. Ikenberry and Mo (2013) note that the challenges South Korea faces in the region are also global challenges and South Korea's response will affect not just peace and stability in the region but also its ability to continue to influencing international affairs generally as a rising "middle power."

3. Perhaps the one exception to this is the years of the Vietnam War which was a strain on relations with the United States and its allies in Northeast Asia.

4. See Chun (2014).

5. This country is now known as Myanmar and its capital city is Yangon.

6. While Pyongyang denied any involvement in this event, an international investigation determined that the Cheonon was sunk by a torpedo from a North Korean submarine.

7. This body of water is referred to as the East Sea in South Korea, a name that is becoming more widely used.

8. Cha (1999) has discussed these differing levels of engagement of the United States up through the 1990s and the impact of these variations on South Korea's relationship with the United States's other ally in the region, Japan. He notes that variations in U.S. engagement levels were significant enough to lead to contrasting entrapment vs. abandonment fears on the part of Tokyo and Seoul, depending on which way the United States's engagement pendulum had swung.

9. This increased engagement in the region by Obama involved two different strategies. The first was known as the "Pivot to Asia" where the United States will increase its engagement in the Asia-Pacific region so it can more effectively promote its interests there as well as those of its allies. The second feature involves a realignment within the Asia-Pacific region, which concerns not just increased U.S. engagement with the nations and multilateral institutions of the Asia Pacific but also a shift away from the United States's traditional emphasis on the security environment of Northeast Asia in favor of more engagement with South and Southeast Asia

10. Naturally, Obama's "Pivot to Asia" did not receive an enthusiastic welcome from China or North Korea.

11. Narrowly defined in this context refers to the current administration defining the quality of an economic relationship the United States has with another nation determined by such things as whether or not the United States runs a bilateral trade deficit with that nation.

12. It is important to remember as Cha (1999) notes that, with respect to South Korea and Japan, this set of triangular relations involves "alignment despite antagonism" that has required careful management from time to time.

13. The second Trump-Kim summit took place in Hanoi in February of 2019 and also ended in failure.

14. The North will also be able to send cultural groups that include an orchestra and an extensive cheering squad.

15. The South Korean delegation did raise the issue at meetings in the demilitarized zone but these questions were met with silence.

16. South Korea also agreed that it would not join a region-wide missile defense system sponsored by the United States.

Appendix

Appendix 1. Descriptive Statistics for Variables

	No. of Obs.	*Mean*	*Standard Deviation*	*Minimum*	*Maximum*
*ln*Korea Dyadic Trade	7017	3.20	3.68	–4.60	12.36
Diplomatic Tie (Embassy)$_{t-1}$	7017	.56	.49	0	1
*ln*Korea GDP$_{t-1}$	7017	11.96	1.90	7.76	14.16
*ln*Partner GDP$_{t-1}$	7017	9.43	2.30	3.60	16.67
Partner's Level of Democracy$_{t-1}$	7017	1.53	7.38	–10	10
Partner's Freedom House Index$_{t-1}$	7017	3.82	1.98	1	7
*ln*Distance	7017	8.63	.49	6.38	9.40
*ln*Korea Population$_{t-1}$	7017	10.62	.18	10.12	10.82
*ln*Partner Population$_{t-1}$	7017	9.01	1.59	4.80	14.12

Bibliography

Ahn, Byung-Joon (1980) "South Korea and the Communist Countries," *Asian Survey*. 20; 11: 1098–1107

Alexandroff, Alan S. and Andrew F. Cooper (Eds.) (2010) *Rising States, Rising Institutions: Can the World be Governed*? Washington, DC: Brookings Institution Press.

Allison, Graham T. and Phillip Zelikow (1999) *Essence of Decision: Explaining the Cuban Missile Crisis*. New York: Longman.

Amsden, Alice (1989) *Asia's Next Giant: South Korea and Late Industrialization*. New York: Oxford University Press.

Baldwin, David A. (1985) *Economic Statecraft*. Princeton, NJ: Princeton University Press.

Bayer, Resat (2006) "Diplomatic Exchange Data Set, v 2006.1" Online: http://www.correlatesofwar.org.

Birdsall, Nancy, Augusto de la Torre, and Felipe Valencia Caicedo (2010) "The Washington Consensus: Assessing a Damaged Brand," *Center for Global Development, Working Paper 211*, May, 2010.

Bishwal, Nisha Desai (2011) "From U.S. Aid Recipient to Donor Partner: The Republic of Korea's Health Ministry Honors USAID," Accessed August 22, 2014. http://blog.usaid.gov/2011/03/fron-u-s-aid-recipient-to-donor-partner—the republic-of-koreas-health-ministry-honors-usaid .

Cha, Victor (1999) *Alignment Despite Antagonism: The U.S.-Korea-Japan Security Triangle*. Stanford, CA: Stanford University Press.

Cha, Victor (2012) *The Impossible State: North Korea, Past and Future*. New York: Harper Collins.

Chun, Hongmin, Elijah N. Munyi and Heejin Lee (2010) South Korea as an Emerging Donor: Challenges and Changes on its Entering OECD/DAC," *Journal of International Development*. 22: 788-802.

Chung, Jae-Ho and Jiyoon Kim (2016) "Is South Korea in China's Orbit? Assessing Seoul's Perceptions and Policies," *Asia Policy*. 21: 123–145.

Chung, Young-Iob (2007) *South Korea in the Fast Lane: Economic Development and Capital Formation.* NY: Oxford University Press.

Chun, Hongmin, Elijah N. Munyi and Heejin Lee (2010) South Korea as an Emerging Donor: Challenges and Changes on its Entering OECD/DAC," *Journal of International Development.* 22: 788–802.

Chung, Young-Iob (2007) *South Korea in the Fast Lane: Economic Development and Capital Formation.* New York: Oxford University Press.

Cooper, Andrew F., Richard A. Higgor, and Kim R. Nossal (1993) *Relocating Middle Powers: Australia and Canada in an changing World.* Vancouver: University of British Columbia Press.

Cooper, Andrew F. (1997) *Niche Diplomacy: Middle Powers after the Cold War.* London: Macmillan.

Cooper, Andrew F. and Daniel Flemes (2013) "Foreign Policy Strategies of Emerging Powers in a Multipolar World: An Introductory Review," *Third World Quarterly.* 34; 6: 943–962.

Cummings, Bruce (1981) *The Origins of the Korean War, Volume 1: Liberation and the Emergence of Separate Regimes.* Princeton, NJ: Princeton University Press.

Cummings, Bruce (1997) *Korea's Place in the Sun: A Modern History*, NY: W.W. Norton.

Diebold, Francis X. (2004) *Elements of Forecasting* (3rd Edition) Mason, OH: Thomson/South-Western.

Eichengren, Barry, Dwight H. Perkins, and Kwangho Shin (2012) *From Miracle to Maturity: The Growth of the Korean Economy.* Cambridge, MA: Harvard University Press.

Ferguson, Shon and Rikard Forslid (2014) "Sizing up the Impact of Embassies on Exports," IFN Working Paper No. 1012, 2014. *Research Institute of Industrial Economics*, Stockholm, Sweden.

Foley, James A. (2003) *Korea's Divided Families: Fifty Years of Separation.* New York: Routledge Curzon.

Fukuyama, Francis (1992) *The End of History and the Last Man.* New York: The Free Press.

Fuqua, Jacques L. (2011) *Korean Unification: Inevitable Challenges.* Washington, DC: Potomac Books.

Giles, Barry K. (1996) *Korea vs. Korea: A Case of Contested Legitimacy.* London: Routledge.

Gu Weiqun. (1995) *Conflicts of Divided Nations: The Cases of China and Korea.* Westport, CT: Praeger.

Ha, Yong-Chul. 2003. *Bukbang Jeongchaek* (North Policy). Seoul, Korea: Seoul National University Press.

Haggard, Stephan, Richard N. Cooper, Susan Collins, Choongsoo Kim, and Sung-Tae Ro (1994) *Macroeconomic Policy and Adjustment in Korea, 1970–1990.* Cambridge, MA: Harvard University Press.

Hamilton, James D. 1994. *Time Series Analysis.* Princeton, NJ: Princeton University Press.

Heo, Uk and Terence Roehrig (2014) *South Korea's Rise: Economic Development, Power, and Foreign Relations*. NY: Cambridge University Press.

Hong, Euny (2014) on the other hand, *The Birth of Korean Cool: How One Nation is Conquering the World through Pop Culture,* NY: Macmillan.

Hurd, Ian (1999) "Legitimacy and Authority in International Politics," *International Organization*. 53; 2: 379–408.

Ikenberry, G. John and Jongryn Mo (2013) *The Rise of Korean Leadership: Emerging Powers and Liberal International Order*. NY: Palgrave Macmillan.

Johnson, Chalmers (1982) *MITI and the Japanese Miracle*. Stanford, CA: Stanford University Press.

Jones, Leroy and Il Sakong (1980) *Government, Business, and Entrepreneurship in Economic Development. The Korean Case*. Cambridge, MA: Harvard University Press.

Kang, David C. (2010) *East Asia before the West: Five Centuries of Trade and Tribute*. NY: Columbia University Press.

Kihl, Young-Whan (1991) "South Korea in 1990: Diplomatic Activism and a Partisan Quagmire," *Asian Survey*. 31; 1: 64–70.

Kihl, Young-Whan and Peter Hayes (Eds.) (1997) *Peace and Security in Northeast Asia: The Nuclear Issue and the Korean Peninsula*.

Kim, Ellen and Victor Cha (2016) "Between a Rock and a Hard Place: South Korea's Strategic Dilemmas with China and the United States," *Asia Policy*. 21: 101–121.

Kim, Eun-Mi and Jinwhan Oh (2012) "Determinants of Foreign Aid: The Case of South Korea," *Journal of East Asian Studies*. 12; 251–273.

Kim, Eun-Mee, Pil Hi Kim, and Jin-Kyung Kim (2013) 'From Development to Development Cooperation: Foreign Aid, Country Ownership, and the Developmental State in South Korea," *The Pacific Review*. 26; 3: 313–336.

Kim, Hak-Joon (1997) "The Process Leading to the Establishment of Diplomatic Relations Between South Korea and the Soviet Union," *Asian Survey*. 37; 7: 637–651.

Kim, Joungwon Alexander (1975) *Divided Korea: The Politics of Development, 1945-1972*. Cambridge MA: Harvard University Press.

Kim Jiyoung (2011) "Foreign Aid and Economic Development: The Success Story of South Korea," *Pacific Focus*. 26; 2: 260–286.

Kim, Ki-Cheon (2010) "The Significance of the Seoul Consensus," *The Chosun Ilbo*. November 16, 2010. Accessed April 23, 2014. http://english.chosun.com/site/data/html_dir/2010/11/16.

Kim, Myung Oak and Sam Jaffe, (2010) *The New Korea: An Inside Look at South Korea's Economic Rise*, NY: AMACOM.

Kim Samuel S. (2000) *Korea's Globalization*. NY: Cambridge University Press.

Kim, Sang-Tae and David Seddon (2005) "ODA Policy and Practice: Japan and the Republic of Korea," in David Arase (ed.) *Japan's Foreign Aid: Old Continuities and New Directions*. London and New York: Routledge.

Kim, Sung Mi (2016) "The Domestic Politics of International Development in South Korea: Stakeholders and Competing Policy Discourses," *The Pacific Review*. 29; 1: 67–91.

Ku, Yamgmo (2018) "Inter-Korean Relations and Reunification," in Yangmo Ku, Inyeop Lee, and Jongseok Woo (Eds.), *Politics in North and South Korea: Political Development, Economy, and Foreign Relations*. New York: Routledge.

Kuznets, Paul W. (1977) *Economic Growth and Structure in the Republic of Korea*. New Haven, CT: Yale University Press.

Lederman, Daniel M., Marcello Olarrega, and Lucy Payton (2010) "Export Promotion Agencies: Do they Work?" *Journal of Development Economics*. 91; 2: 257–265.

Lee, Chae-Jin (2006) *A Troubled Peace: U.S. Policy and the Two Koreas*. Baltimore, MD: Johns Hopkins University Press.

Lee, Chong-Sik (1963) "Korea: In Search of Stability," *Asian Survey*. 4; 1: 656–665.

Lee, Sook-Jong, (2012) "South Korea as New Middle Power Seeking Complex Diplomacy," EAI Asia Security Initiative, Working Paper No. 25. Seoul South Korea: East Asia Institute,

Lumley, Thomas and Patrick Heagerty. 1999. Weighted Empirical Adaptive Variance Estimators for Correlated Data Regression. *Journal of the Royal Statistical Society* B 61(2): 459–477.

Mearsheimer, John (1990) "Back to the Future: Instability in Europe after the Cold War," *International Security*. 15; 1: 5–56.

Ministry of Foreign Affairs and Trade (2012) *2012 Diplomatic White Paper*. Seoul: Ministry of Foreign Affairs and Trade.

Ministry of Foreign Affairs and Trade (MOFAT). 2013. Diplomatic Missions Established by Year (in Korean). Accessed September 20, 2013. http://www.index.go.kr/egams/stts/jsp/potal/stts/PO_STTS_IdxSearch.jsp?idx_cd=1676&stts_cd=167601&clas_div=&idx_sys_cd=&idx_clas_cd=1.

Miskovic, Natasa, Harold Fischer-Tine, and Nada Boskovska (Eds.) (2014) *The Non-Aligned Movement and the Cold War*. London: Routledge.

Mo, Jongryn and Barry Weingast (2013) *Korean Political and Economic Development*. Cambridge, MA: Harvard University Press.

Newnham, Randall E. (2002) "Embassies for Sale: The Purchase of Diplomatic Recognition by West Germany, Taiwan, and South Korea," *International Politics*. 37: 259–284.

Nitsch, Volker (2007) "State Visits and International Trade," *The World Economy*. 30; 12: 1797–1816.

Nohlen, Dieter, Florian Grotz, and Christof Hartmann (2001) *Elections in Asia and the Pacific: A Data Handbook*, Volume II. London: Oxford University Press.

North, Douglas, John Joseph Wallis, and Barry Weingast (2009) *Violence and Social Orders: A Conceptual Framework for Interpreting Recorded Human History*. Cambridge, UK: Cambridge University Press.

OECD (2012) *Korea: Development Assistance Committee, Peer Review, 2012*. Paris: Organization for Economic Cooperation and Development.

OECD (2017) *OECD Glossary of Statistical Terms*. Accessed August 14, 2016. http://stats.oecd.org/glossary/detail.asp?ID=6043.

Oh, Jinhwan (2014) "Mutual Priority and Aid Effectiveness: Is South Korea a Major Donor to Its Major Recipients?" *Pacific Focus*. 29; 1: 116–139.

Park, Kun-Young (Ed.) (2014) *Inter-Korean Relations: Family of Enemy?* Seoul, SK: Hollym Corp.

Park, Kyung-Ae and Scott Snyder (Eds.) (2013) *North Korea in Transition: Politics, Economy, and Society*. Lanham, MD: Rowman & Littlefield.

Pollins, Brian (1989a) "Does Trade Still Follow the Flag?" *American Political Science Review*. 83; 2: 465–480.

Pollins, Brian (1989b) "Conflict, Cooperation, and Commerce: The Effect of International Political Interactions on Bilateral Trade Flows," *American Journal of Political Science*.

Reeve, W. D. (1963) *The Republic of Korea: A Political and Economic Study*. London: Oxford University Press.

Riddell, Roger C. (2008) *Does Foreign Aid Really Work*? New York: Oxford University Press.

Roehrig, Terence (2013) "South Korea, Foreign Aid, and UN Peacekeeping: Contributing to International Peace and Security as a Middle Power," *Korea Observer*. 44; 4: 623–645.

Rogowski, Ronald. (1989) *Commerce and Coalitions: How Trade Affects Domestic Political Alignments*. Princeton: Princeton University Press.

Rose, Andrew K. (2007) "The Foreign Service and Foreign Trade: Embassies as Export Promotion," *The World Economy*. 30; 1: 22–38.

Rozman, Gilbert (2003) "Northeast Asia: The Geopolitics of The Korean Nuclear Crisis," in Richard J. Ellings and Aaron Friedberg (Eds.) *Strategic Asia 2003-04: Fragility and Crisis*. Seattle, WA: National Bureau of Asian Research.

Seth, Michael J. (2011) *A History of South Korea: From Antiquity to Present*. Lanham, MD: Rowman & Littlefield.

Singer, J. David and Melvin Small (1966) "The Composition and Status Ordering of the International System, 1815–1940," *World Politics*. 18; 2: 236–282.

Small, Melvin and J. David Singer (1973) "The Diplomatic Importance of States, 1816-1970," *World Politics*. 25; 4: 577–599.

Snyder, Scott A. (2018) *South Korea at the Crossroads: Autonomy and Alliance in an Era of Rival Powers*. New York: Columbia University Press.

Sohn, Hyuk-Sang and Nari Yoo (2015) "Motivation for Aid Allocation and Political Ideology: A Case Study of South Korea," *Pacific Focus*. 30; 3: 344–371.

Steinberg, David I. (1985) *Foreign Aid and the Development of the Republic of Korea: The Effectiveness of Concessional Assistance*, AID Special Study No. 42. Washington, DC: Agency for International Development

Stolper, Wolfgang Friedrich and Paul A. Samuelson. (1941) "Protection and Real Wages." *Review of Economic Studies*. 9: 58–73.

Waltz, Kenneth (1979) *Theory of International Politics*. New York: McGraw Hill.

Woo, Jongseok (2018) "North Korean Ideology and Politics," in Yangmo Ku, Inyeop Lee, and Jongseok Woo, (Eds.) *Politics in North and South Korea: Political Development, Economy, and Foreign Relations*. New York: Routledge.

Wooldridge, Jeffrey M. (2013) *Introductory Econometrics: A Modern Approach* (5th edition). Mason, OH: South-Western.

World Bank. 2013. World Development Indicators. Accessed September 1, 2013. http://data.worldbank.org/products/data-portals.

Ye Min (2018) *China-South Korea Relations in the New Era*. Latham, MD: Lexington Books.

Index

About the Authors

Dennis Patterson received his PhD from the University of California, Los Angeles in Political Science. He has lived in Japan and has been conducting research in Japan and South Korea of over thirty years. He has over forty published articles, and this class is currently on his sixth book, which addresses the importance of the East Asian Alliance in the context of a rising China. He has been a professor at Texas Tech University for sixteen years and previously taught at Michigan State University and the University of Wisconsin, Milwaukee.

Jangsup Choi is associate professor of political science at Texas A&M University-Commerce. His research interests involve political behavior, campaigns and elections, and Asian politics, with special attention to the decision-making process and political outcomes largely influenced by institutional arrangements. His recent publications have been appeared on *Politics and Religion, Studies in Ethnicity and Nationalism, Islam and Christian-Muslim Relations, Korea Journal, Korea Observer*, and *The Korean Journal of Area Studies*.

www.ingramcontent.com/pod-product-compliance
Lightning Source LLC
Chambersburg PA
CBHW051251200926
51612CB00001B/5
9781498583084